MW01071225

The Mughal Empire and British Raj

A Captivating Guide to the History of India, Starting from the Mughals to the British Empire

Free Bonus from Captivating History (Available for a Limited time)

Hi History Lovers!

Now you have a chance to join our exclusive history list so you can get your first history ebook for free as well as discounts and a potential to get more history books for free! Simply visit the link below to join.

Captivatinghistory.com/ebook

Also, make sure to follow us on Facebook, Twitter and Youtube by searching for Captivating History.

Contents

Part 1: The Mughal Empire

A Captivating Guide to the Mughal Empire in South Asia and the Impact the Mughals Had on the History of India

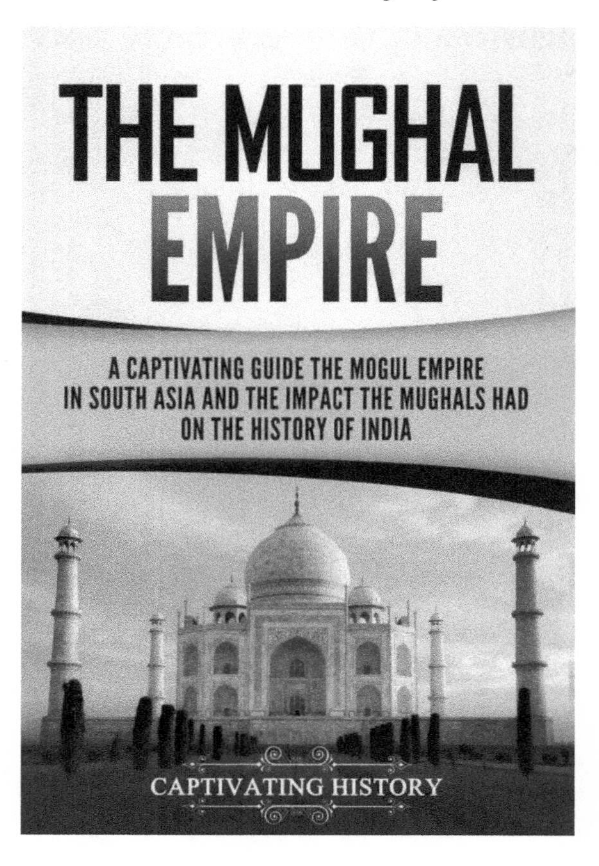

Introduction

The Mughal Empire, also known as the Moghul Empire, lasted for about three centuries, and at its peak, it covered 3.2 million square kilometers, from the outer borders of the Indus Basin in the west to the highlands of Assam and Bangladesh in the east, and from Afghanistan and Kashmir in the north to the Deccan Plateau in the south. The Mughal Empire also took the territories of what used to be known as Hindustan in the northern Indian subcontinent. With such a large territory came many diverse peoples, roughly numbering 150 million souls. The name "Mughal" comes from the Persian word for Mongols, which, over time, came to mean only the Islamic people of Babur's dynasty in India.

During its peak, the Mughal Empire was one of humanity's most powerful and richest political entities, overshadowed maybe only by contemporary China. The empire relied on its military, and as such, most of its income was spent on supplying and maintaining the most modern army of the period. The rulers relied on conquest, which would reward the most loyal soldiers and bring new lands and people who would farm it. The Mughal Empire mostly owes the success of its army to its visionary founders, who employed foreign gunpowder experts that helped to bring destruction upon their enemies. The power of the early Mughal Empire was unmatched in the whole of

India, and once the father of the empire, Babur, started conquering the lands, there was no stopping them.

The origins of the Mughal Empire can be found in the Muslim territories of Central Asia, and even though they were not the first Islamic rulers of northern India, they were certainly newcomers who had to adapt and overcome additional difficulties compared to the native rulers. Even though the land was rich with people and fertile grounds, it was completely new to Babur and his Central Asian warriors. As foreigners, they had to face many uprisings from the domesticated Muslims and Hindus, who defied bowing to rulers coming from distant lands. It took generations for the Mughals to settle in their new lands and take full control over the diverse peoples that eventually became their new subjects.

The Mughals, as well as the Mongols, whom the Mughals originated from, were considered to be uncultured yet fierce warriors. During their three-century rule in northern India, the Mughals transformed from a warrior tribe to one of the most sophisticated empires, developing court etiquettes and promoting the fine arts. The empire turned from fierce conquerors to becoming the center of the Indian world, and many people came here for education or to practice their crafts. The Mughal Empire was never an indigenous national empire, and it never had a mono-ethnic army. The Mughals were always diverse peoples who found a way to coexist with other cultures in very demanding times.

However, the Mughal Empire continued expanding to the point where it could only break. The administration eventually failed, with uprisings destroying the fringes of the empire, and it began its downfall, which would last for one and a half centuries. In the end, it was led by a series of weak rulers who were unable to hold the empire together. Like sand running through their fingers, the empire was lost bit by bit. Both Indian and European challengers dismantled it completely, leaving only the city of Old Delhi as a remembrance of the once glorious empire. Finally, in 1857, the Mughal Empire was no more, and the descendants of a once royal dynasty were dispersed through the Indian subcontinent, living the lives of commoners.

Chapter 1 – Origins of the Mughal Empire

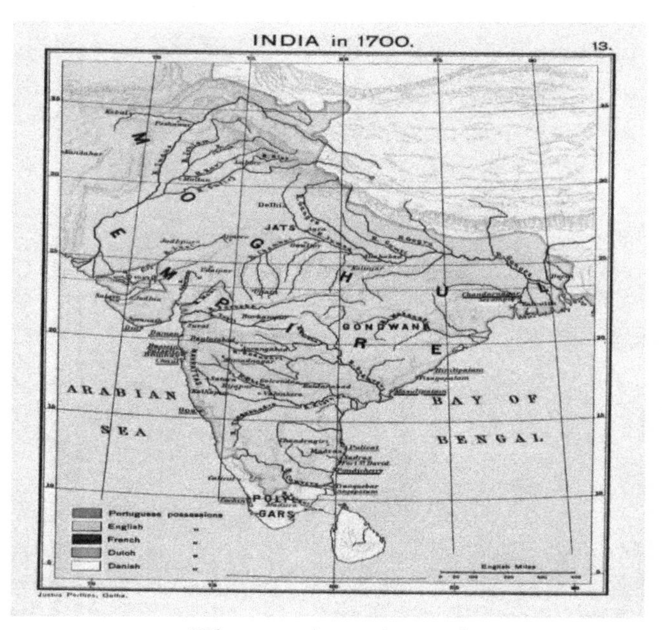

The empire at its peak

https://en.wikipedia.org/wiki/Mughal_Empire#/media/File:Joppen1907India1700a.jpg

On March 4th, 1519, the son of martial adventurer and ruler of Kabul Babur, was born. He was named Hindal, Taker of India, since Hindal was born in the same year Babur requested the submission of Ibrahim, the young sultan of Delhi. To persuade Ibrahim to submit, Babur sent him gifts and an ultimatum. But those didn't work on the young sultan, whose family had ruled northern India for generations in a territory known as Hindustan. Babur claimed the right to rule northern India because his ancestor, Timur, had conquered Delhi a century earlier. But those Indians who were familiar with the name of Timur, few as they were, were weary as they had only heard the stories of his raids and the devastation he brought to the land.

Ibrahim's governor in Lahore denied access to Babur and his small war party, and he didn't even bother to notify the sultan of his arrival. In his memoirs, known as the *Baburnama,* Babur complained that the people of Hindustan had no wisdom as they didn't dare to stand against their enemies, nor did they know how to respond to the act of friendship. Thus declined, this Central Asian martial adventurer could only return home to enjoy his newborn son. However, seven years later, he would invade Hindustan and kill the young Sultan Ibrahim. With this conquest, Babur came to possess the royal treasuries of the former sultanate, which were rich enough to give him power over the whole region. The Mughal Empire was thus born.

Babur (r. 1526–1530)

Babur, the first emperor of the Mughal Empire

https://en.wikipedia.org/wiki/Babur#/media/File:Babur_of_India.jpg

Babur's true name was Zahir-ud-Din, which means "Defender of Faith" in Arabic. His date of birth was recorded as being on February 14th, 1483, in Andijan, which is in today's Uzbekistan. On his father's side, he was a descendant of Timur of the Timurid Empire. On his mother's side, he was a direct descendant of Genghis Khan of the Mongol Empire. With ancestors like that, it is no wonder Babur strived to rule his whole life. He was the eldest son of the ruler of the Fergana Valley, Umar Shaikh Mirza II of the Barlas tribe. The title of mirza was often used by the leaders of various Persian tribes, such as Babur's father, but later, it would transform, and only the princes of the royal family of the Mughals would be honored with the title, as well as some distinguished military commanders. The Barlas tribe was of Mongolian origin, but they did embrace Turkic and Persian culture as their identity and Islam as their faith. Scholars believe that because of this mixture of cultures, specifically Mongolian and

Arabic, Babur was able to gain the support of many people from Central Asia, especially Iranians and those of Turkic origin. His army was ethnically diverse as it included Persians, Arabs, Afghans, Barlas, and other Turko-Mongol tribes of Central Asia. It is believed that his true name, Zahir-ud-Din, was too complicated to pronounce for his multiethnic army and that it was them who gave him the nickname Babur, a Persian word that means "tiger."

In 1494, when he was only eleven years old, Babur's father died. However, even at that young age as a ruler, Babur managed to secure his rightful place as the leader of the Fergana Valley. However, his position was threatened by his own uncles, and they weren't the only ones who threatened the boy's position. A part of the people he now ruled believed that his younger brother, Jahangir, would be a more formidable leader. It is important to understand that the Central Asian peoples did not follow the usual primogeniture laws of inheritance, where the rule is passed from the father to his eldest son. As long as the male child was recognized as legitimate, he had the right to inherit the rule. As such, it wasn't unusual in Central Asia to see brothers at war with each other. Babur had the help of his grandmother, Aisan Daulat Begum. She was his mother's mother and the first wife of Yunus Khan of Moghulistan. All of this contributed to a dynastic turmoil, which was common within the ruling families. As warrior peoples, these clans were constantly at conflict, and after the passing of Babur's father, they saw an opportunity to gain new territories.

This is this cultural setting in which Babur grew up in, and when he was fifteen, he planned his first military conquest. He wanted to conquer Samarkand, a city that lay in the Bukhara region. For the next seven months, his army besieged the city. The losses were heavy on both sides, but Babur managed to gain the submission of the neighboring forts. While moving his army from one position to the other, the citizens of Samarkand wrongly thought he was retreating, and they decided to attack. They sent their soldiers outside of the city, and Babur had the opportunity to confront them on the open field. Finally, he was able to show off his military power, and his cavalry overran the army of Samarkand.

However, the city still endured, and winter was fast approaching. Unwilling to leave the territory, Babur decided to spend the winter with his army in one of the forts that submitted to him. This pause of the siege allowed Baysonqor Mirza, the sultan of Bukhara, to ask Muhammad Shaybani, an Uzbek warrior, for help. He led his army of around three thousand men to Samarkand, where he met Babur for the first time—Shaybani would later become a true nemesis of Babur. However, disappointed by the cold reception he encountered in the city of Samarkand, Shaybani left after only a few days.

Seeing that his last hope, the Uzbek army, was gone, Baysonqor Mirza abandoned the city and his kingdom. With a small retinue of followers, he left for Afghanistan. When their leader left, the citizens of Samarkand had no other choice than to surrender to the one who had besieged them, and Babur finally took the city without any opposition. Samarkand used to be the capital of Emperor Timur, and in the 16th century, it continued to be one of the biggest, richest, and most respected cities. And now, fifteen-year-old Babur ruled it.

However, the long siege cost the city, and there was not enough plunder for Babur's army, so many soldiers deserted due to lack of payment. There was not enough food for the citizens either, and the fertile fields outside of the city weren't plowed. Farmers had no seeds to plant, making the upcoming harvest difficult. As if the troubles in Samarkand weren't enough, back home in the Fergana Valley, the nobles who supported his brother rebelled, and Jahangir Mirza was proclaimed the new king. With the few troops he was left with, Babur marched to reclaim his kingdom. But since the troops were dissatisfied, they eventually left him. Babur was now without an army, without Samarkand, and without his kingdom.

So, for the next three years, Babur gathered an army. He recruited troops from all the ethnicities of Central Asia. Finally, once his army was strong enough, he launched another attack on

Samarkand. And his siege was successful, as he managed to take and rule it for almost one hundred days.

But his rival Muhammad Shaybani was back with no intention to leave. This time, he wanted to conquer the city for himself, not for a sultan who treated him as an inferior. During the three years that Babur had spent gathering his army, Shaybani led a series of successful campaigns with which he gained power among the Uzbeks. In 1500/01, Babur had to negotiate for peace. The situation was indeed very bad as he not only had to offer his sister Khanzada Begum's hand in marriage to Muhammad Shaybani, but he also had to leave the city. Babur had nowhere to go, so he decided to try and take his old kingdom back, the Fergana Valley. But his army, already tired and decimated by the fighting at Samarkand, stood no chance to win back Fergana. In fact, Babur lost everything but his life. With a small group of warriors, he escaped and tried to find his luck in Tashkent, a city ruled by one of his uncles. However, he wasn't welcomed there, and he wrote in his memoirs how he was often humiliated by his uncle and his court. He lived in poverty, and he only survived due to the compassion of his friends and strangers. Only ten years after gaining control over Fergana, Babur was now a prince in exile.

One of Babur's paternal uncles ruled Kabul, but he died in 1501, leaving an opportunity for the prince in exile to reclaim his throne, as the only heir of Kabul was just an infant. However, a rivaling Timurid prince was quicker in seizing the city, marrying the daughter of the previous ruler to make his conquest legitimate. But that didn't help, as he was still seen as a usurper, and the people he ruled resented him. When Babur gathered an army of 200 loyal followers, the people of Kabul welcomed him as a savior. After all, he was the nephew to their previous ruler, which gave him all the legitimacy he needed. With ease, Babur dispatched the usurper and started ruling his newly gained kingdom.

In 1506, Babur allied himself with his cousin, Sultan Husayn Mirza Bayqara of Herat, and their intention was to attack

Muhammad Shaybani together. However, Bayqara died the same year, and his sons didn't want to go to war. Babur stayed in Herat for the next two months, as it was the capital of eastern Muslim culture at the time. There, he learned about history and language, which inspired him to start writing his memoirs. After Babur left, the city of Herat was conquered by Shaybani, and Bayqara's sons were killed. Babur was now the most powerful ruler of the Timurid dynasty, and as such, he started calling himself Padshah, meaning the "Great King" or "Emperor." Many relatives and princes of the neighboring regions sought shelter in Kabul, as Shaybani ravaged their lands. The ancestral lands of the Timurid dynasty were now all conquered by the Uzbek leader Shaybani, who became a real threat to Kabul.

Some princes and nobles of Kabul didn't believe Babur would be able to protect them from the attacks of the Uzbeks, and they organized a rebellion. However, Babur was able to quell it pretty quickly. Two years later, though, another rebellion started, and this time, the military generals of Kabul managed to expel Babur. However, Babur still had loyal friends in the city who advocated for him, and the leaders of the rebels switched to his side, allowing Babur to take over the city once more.

In the meantime, Shaybani was killed in 1510 during the conflict he had with Ismail I, the shah of Shia Safavid Persia. Uzbek power was diminishing, and Babur allied himself with Shah Ismail to regain his ancestral territories of Central Asia. In 1513, he left for Samarkand to lay siege to it for the third time. There, he was reunited with his sister, who had been forced to marry Babur's enemy Shaybani. Babur ruled Samarkand for the next three years, but in 1514, he returned to Kabul after he lost Samarkand to the Uzbeks for the third time.

Babur spent the next eleven years ruling in relative peace. He took the time to reorganize his army in preparation for the conquest of Hindustan, and he carried out small raids in the territory of northern India and successfully dealt with small rebellions in the area of modern Afghanistan. Even though the regions were relatively peaceful, Babur undertook the long and demanding task of modernizing his army.

Formation of the Empire

The Uzbeks remained a threat, and as Babur records in his memoirs, he wanted to put some space between his people and their enemies. Although some of his people found refuge in Badakhshan, just north of Kabul, Babur looked to India, as it was a much farther and safer place. Since Babur had lost Samarkand, he chose to dedicate himself to conquering the territories of India. As a first step, he started reorganizing his fractured army. In 1519, he was ready to embark on his first campaign to today's Pakistan. Following the footsteps of his predecessor Timur, Babur wanted to spread his influence to Punjab, as these regions used to be a part of the Timurid Empire.

At this time, parts of northern India were ruled by Sultan Ibrahim of the Lodi dynasty. However, Ibrahim's rule was weak, and his empire deteriorated. Many of the followers of the Indian sultan decided to switch sides and join Babur. It was at this point that Babur sent an ambassador with gifts to the young sultan asking him to recognize Babur as his supreme ruler. However, the ambassador was detained in Lahore and didn't even see the sultan. Instead, he spent many months as a prisoner.

In 1524, Babur started his main campaign to take over Punjab, but he was met there by the forces of Ibrahim Lodi, which had disposed of his uncle, Daulat Khan Lodi, the ruler of Punjab. In Lahore, the armies met, and the Lodi army was forced to retreat, but Babur wasn't satisfied by this turn of events. Instead, he burned the city for the next two days and then installed Alam Khan, another rebellious uncle of Ibrahim Lodi, as the governor. Alam lost the city once Babur left with his army, and he had to run to Kabul. There, he was met by Babur's army, who helped him reach his brother, Daulat Khan Lodi. Together, Ibrahim's uncles besieged Delhi. However, the young sultan easily defeated the united army, and Babur realized that Punjab would be much harder to conquer then he initially thought.

During the year 1525, Babur was staying in Peshawar, a trade center on the route between India and Central Asia. There, he received news that Daulat Khan Lodi had abandoned him and joined his nephew, Sultan Ibrahim. Babur decided to confront Daulat Khan, and he marched his troops to what is known to history as the First Battle of Panipat. After Babur crossed the Indus River in November 1526 and entered Punjab with his mighty army, Daulat Khan surrendered without a fight as his army abandoned him upon seeing the force of Babur. Daulat Khan was pardoned once he granted the rule over Punjab to Babur. The army continued on, and on April 20th, 1526, they reached Panipat, which was only 90 kilometers (almost 56 miles) away from Delhi, where the army of Sultan Ibrahim Lodi was waiting.

Babur records that Ibrahim's army was superior. It numbered 100,000 soldiers and 100 elephants against Babur's 15,000 men. But the numbers didn't deter Babur; instead, he devised a plan. He used the city of Panipat as protection for his right flank. A trench was also dug out and covered with branches to hide it to serve as a defense for the left flank of the army. In the center, between the city and the trench, Babur placed 700 carts that were tied together with ropes, and they served as a defense for the artillery. This was essential to protect, as his modernized army relied on the use of gunpowder, as he employed Turkish cannon specialists and had created the matchlock infantry. Babur's army was placed between the city and the trench, and those defenses created a narrow approach for Ibrahim's soldiers.

The sultan was forced to reorganize his army, as he had hoped for an open field battle. Babur took the opportunity of Ibrahim's confusion to deploy a tactic known as *tulughma*, in which he split his army into smaller units and created front and rear flanks. Because his army was much smaller than Ibrahim's, his only chance was to surround the enemy from all sides. Ibrahim relied heavily on his elephants and cavalry, but Babur had modernized his army and used cannons against them. Two flanks, a side and a rear, attacked Lodi's army, massacring them. Both sides suffered heavy losses, but Babur was able to win the battle in just three hours against a much stronger enemy by using a mixture of Ottoman and Mongolian tactics. Sultan Ibrahim Lodi was killed during the battle, and thus, the Delhi Sultanate ceased to exist.

Babur was now the ruler of northern India, and by taking the territories that used to belong to the Lodi dynasty, he set the foundations for his future Mughal Empire. But he was challenged by neighboring magnates who wanted to take advantage of the opportunity of regional instability and take Lodi's throne for themselves. Before setting in motion the construction of his empire, he had to defeat these new challengers, especially one named Rana Sanga, the ruler of Mewar. Rana is the title used only by absolute Hindu monarchs. It is equivalent to an emperor, unlike raja, which is equivalent to a king. In this context, the title of maharaja can be translated as "high king" and was also used like the European title "the Great," such as Alexander the Great or Alfred the Great. The two armies met at the Battle of Khanwa on March 17th, 1527.

Rana Sanga recognized the strength of his enemy Babur, and to fight him, he allied with all the kings of Rajasthan, a state of northern India, who either joined the battle personally or sent a contingent of soldiers. The alliance also included Mahmud Lodi, the younger brother of Ibrahim Lodi. He was proclaimed the sultan of the Afghans shortly after his brother's death, and he brought 10,000 of his soldiers to the battle. Hasan Khan Mewati, the ruler of Mewat, brought 12,000 soldiers. Others who joined the army were rulers of the various cities of Rajasthan, including Harauti, Dungarpur, Dhundhar, Jalor, and Sirohi. The Rajput-Afghan alliance had a mission of expelling Babur, who was seen as a Turkic intruder from the Lodi empire.

Babur's memoirs record Rana Sanga's army numbering 200,000 men. However, historians consider this number to be an exaggeration and believe that the Rajput army had only 40,000 soldiers. However, this exaggeration most likely means that the alliance had a much larger army than Babur, no matter what the real numbers were. As Babur's army was outnumbered once more, his men suffered from low morale, and to raise it, Babur gave a religious meaning to the battle. He proclaimed that he would live in total abstinence from wine from that day forward. He even broke all his drinking cups and spilled all the liquor on the ground to show his intentions were sincere. His actions not only impacted his army but his enemies as well.

The battle took place on March 16th, 1527, near Khanwa in the Agra District of Uttar Pradesh. Babur reused the tactics from the previous battle in Panipat, as he used carts to create a defense for his artillery. His matchlock infantry hid behind wheeled shields made out of rawhide stretched on tripods. This way, they would have protection, and they could easily advance or retreat. With further modernization of his army, Babur had no difficulty defeating his enemy, who fought in the traditional way. Yet again, he surrounded the enemy army and ordered his artillery and matchlocks to advance. The carts, which protected the artillery, were pushed forward, and the cannons followed. The allied army of Rana Sanga fought hard, but Raja Shiladitya of northeastern Malwa deserted and took his soldiers to Babur's side. Rana was defeated, and to show his disrespect toward his enemy, Babur ordered a tower of enemy skulls to be built. These towers were common Ottoman tactics of frightening their adversaries, but they also served as memorials to the battles.

Rana Sanga escaped the battlefield alive, and he found refuge in Chittor, but the alliance he built collapsed after this battle, never again to be united against their common enemy. Scholars comment that Rana Sanga would have probably defeated Babur if there were no cannons in Babur's artillery, as Rana held the superiority in numbers, not to mention the famous bravery of the Rajput soldiers. Rana died the next year, in late January 1528, in Chittor. He wanted to confront Babur once more, but his generals considered such a move to be suicide. Instead of openly opposing him, they decided to poison him.

However, the word that Rana planned to renew the conflict reached Babur, and he decided to attack one of the allied forces, Medini Rai, the ruler of eastern Malwa. He hoped that by defeating the allies of Rana Sanga, he would be able to isolate Rana Sanga and deal with him easily. So, Babur marched his army to Chanderi in January of 1528, which fell after just two days. To avoid capture and enslavement, the women and children of Chanderi committed the ritual of Jauhar, a self-immolation ceremony.

Chapter 2 – In the New Land

Difficulties of the New Empire

Babur founded the Mughal Empire for his Central Asian followers. However, they were all new to the region and found themselves ruling over people who spoke different languages and had different cultures, religions, and values. Babur was an alien to the Hindustan he now ruled, and his new subjects did not speak Persian or the Turkic language of Babur's followers. Not even the Afghans who inhabited this part of the world spoke these languages. As a foreign emperor, Babur was an intruder in the eyes of the people of Hindustan. They regarded him as an illegitimate ruler who had invaded them. Because of it, Babur had to rely on his military power to rule over his new subjects.

In order to maintain his expensive army, Babur had to reward the commanders and pay the soldiers. But since his empire was new, he didn't have a proper land taxation system. To finance his army, Babur had to capture the royal treasures of neighboring cities. However, this meant the constant expansion of his empire, for which he had no resources. Each year, he had to launch campaigns in the neighboring provinces, which, one by one, submitted to his rule, from the east where the Sultanate of Bengal ruled to the west where the nomadic rulers of the Baloch people lived. All these conquered peoples agreed to pay a yearly tribute to Babur, but only while they were under immediate threat. As soon as the Mughal army retreated, they would stop sending money, treasures, food, and other resources.

The cities that resisted the longest were always given to Babur's Central Asian commanders. These cities were extorted, as they had to pay for the army's maintenance, including their pleasures, but they also had to send a yearly tribute to Babur's personal treasury. However, the commanders who ruled these cities were strangers, and they often had a hard time finding a common language with the locals, who took every opportunity to disobey their invaders. Commanders were often too frightened to take up residency inside the city, choosing to set up their quarters in the military garrisons outside the city walls instead. In addition, Babur would often recall his commanders when he needed them for new military campaigns, and there was no one left to gather the tribute from these cities. Babur would also relocate his commanders too often, which wouldn't allow the commanders to make any kind of bond with the locals and convince them of the intentions for the newly formed empire.

Babur's army was modernized with guns and cannons. Thus, it was a very expensive army to maintain. It was this modernization and use of gunpowder that allowed Babur to successfully capture Hindustan, as his opponents fought in the traditional way without access to gunpowder and new military technologies. Babur was employing Ottoman gunpowder experts, the most prominent among them being Master Ustad Ali Quli and Mustafa Rumi Khan. Both of them came from Constantinople or what Central Asians called *Rumi*, meaning second Rome. This is why Mustafa's title was "Rumi Khan," to indicate his importance. This title would later be given to other artillery commanders who distinguished themselves in Babur's military campaigns.

The cannons Babur paid so expensively for were indeed powerful, and they helped immensely in conquering Hindustan. However, they had some limitations. They were long-ranged weapons, perfect for use when the target was across a river or stationed within a citadel. But they did not have enough power to breach the walls of large cities unless the cannons were positioned on higher ground. Also, the cannons needed a long cooling time in between shots, as the barrel could easily crack if overheated. The maximum number of shots of Babur's cannons was sixteen per day. It wasn't that bad of a number considering how powerful they were. But, on the other hand, they weren't reliable. The mortar would shatter and wound or even kill his own soldiers. The cannons were also very large, and they needed to be pulled by elephants. Babur had to cut down whole jungles to make roads for the transportation of these cannons, which was mostly considered to be a major time-waster.

The cavalry and infantry of Babur's army were the most easily maintained. Cavalry was often rewarded with local lands, which their families could live and work on. Infantry was easily dismissed and called back to service. But the gunpowder experts had to stay in Babur's employment, and he had to finance them regularly, often from his own treasuries. Because of the number of valuable soldiers who wielded muskets and cannons, Babur emptied Sultan Ibrahim's treasuries after only two years of ruling his new Mughal Empire. The commanders he assigned as governors of the conquered cities were pressed to send him more and more revenue, which further created mistrust from the local populace.

The people of Hindustan weren't the only problems Babur's new empire encountered. The environment of northern India wasn't the same as in their homelands in Central Asia. The extreme temperatures and the rainfall variations of the monsoon seasons were all new to Babur's followers. Even though the heartland of the Mughal Empire was all fertile land, they lacked rain during the whole year. And the outskirts of the empire in Rajasthan and the Indus plains were close to the environment of a desert. The Central Asians were used to drylands; however, they weren't prepared for the high temperatures of India. In the winter, the monsoon season would hit the northern parts of India once more, making it possible for the Mughals in the heartland to have a second harvest, but the other parts of the empire would experience drought and a lack of food. Since Babur was relying on military campaigns to finance his empire, the land was often at war, and the transportation of food to the hunger-stricken areas was often disrupted.

Religion and Culture

Babur didn't have enough Central Asian commanders who he could employ as governors or in other positions of his administration. So, he began to recruit Indians for his army and court, but they would only be given commanding posts and higher offices if they were Muslims. Most of the recruits were Shaikhzadas, Indians whose ancestors had converted to Islam much earlier. Northern India was also home to many Afghans who had settled there a few centuries earlier, and they were also welcomed in the ranks of Babur's army and court.

Non-Muslims were either given positions of subordinate officers, common soldiers, workers, or scribes. Some of them even previously served Sultan Ibrahim, but Babur needed them, as they were experienced and well-informed. They were also valuable workers, as they were natives, and their roots were from the land he now ruled. They were a source of information for Babur, as they knew the revenues each city was paying to Ibrahim and what could potentially be exploited from the new regions his army would conquer. Because Babur started employing Hindu scribes and administrative workers, his court was attractive enough for thousands of Indian artists, masons, and servants to flock to his empire, who found employment at his court or in the households of his

commanders.

Babur was spiritually tied to Sufism, a form of Islamic mysticism that followed the precepts set by the prophet Muhammad. More correctly, he belonged to the Naqshbandi order, just like his ancestor Timur. The Naqshbandi traced its spiritual lineage to Muhammad through his father-in-law, Abu Bakr, unlike other orders that do it through the prophet's close relatives. It was the principles of this Islamic order that Babur set as the main spiritual support of his whole regime. Any member of the Naqshbandi was a prominent courtier of Emperor Babur. His devotion to the order is probably best displayed through his vow to versify *Risala-i Walidiyya*, which was written by Pir Khwaja, a long-dead Naqshbandi Sufi master. The poem had 243 lines, and Babur even claimed that it was these verses that helped him overcome his constant desire for wine.

However, as the emperor of the Mughals, Babur started honoring the India-based Sufi masters, such as the Shattari or Suhrawardi pirs. To clarify, the word pir, in the context of Islam, is used as a title for spiritual leaders. Sultan Ibrahim granted revenues to the religious institutions that honored these pirs, and when Babur started his rule over the northern Indian territories, he renewed the revenue streams. He often invested in other Sufi orders that had a wide network of religious institutions across India. By doing so, Babur reinforced the legitimacy of his rule, and he ensured that religious leaders would support his descendants. However, many of the pirs fought each other for religious and political supremacy, and they vied for Babur's financial support.

Through Babur's memoirs, there is a strong sense of the ambivalence about settling in Hindustan. Even so, he remained open-minded toward all the new experiences India brought to him and his Central Asian followers. He was particularly fascinated by the diversity of nature and animal life in India, as well as the artistry of Indian masons and monuments. In his autobiography, Babur explained in detail the measurement systems used across India, but he never paid enough attention to its peoples and their cultures. However, he did express his shock that Indian peasants, both male and female, went around half-naked due to the heat of the regions. He also couldn't grasp the artistic value of India's nude sculptures, and a large number of these were destroyed on his orders. Some scholars believe Babur was too prude and that he was not motivated by religion when he ordered the destruction of the nude statues in Gwalior.

Though he might have been prude, he didn't shy away from the pleasurable places he discovered or built himself. He was famous for building many gardens in the Central Asian style, which would shelter him and his followers from the discomfort of India. He was always bothered by the hot, dry air and dust in some of the regions of his empire, and he was in a constant search for suitable places where he could build pleasure refuges. Since his court was nomadic, Babur's whole household would move from one region to another. Because of that, he needed a network of walled residences with these elaborate gardens that would protect him from the elements of the Indian subcontinent. In his *Baburnama*, he described his shock at the low cost of Indian masons and artisans, whom he employed to build these gardens. He also complimented their skill and their numbers, but he never named one individual. Babur always referred to them in the plural and by their profession. Because he was constantly closed behind walls with his Central Asian commanders, he created even more distance between himself and the locals. This is why his walled residences were nicknamed "Kabul" by the Indian populace, who had nothing in common with their ruler.

Babur's Mughal Empire was a vast territory. As such, it was rich in culture, but it was also rich in gold and silver. Babur displayed mixed feelings about living in Hindustan. He was attracted to its riches, but he hated its climate. In his writings, he even admits he was seduced by the wealth India brought but that he hated the land. Although he would sometimes display enjoyment in what India had to offer, he often longed for the more pleasing climate of Central Asia.

Succession and the End of the Life of Babur

Babur ruled his Mughal Empire for only four years. In Hindustan, his health constantly declined. At one point, because of his fragile health, some noblemen conspired against his sons for the succession. They wanted to install another nobleman, who was also a descendant of Timur, as the ruler of the Mughals. His name was Mir

Muhammad Mahdi Khwaja, and he was the new husband of Babur's sister Khanzada Begum. However, since the empire he created was a patrimonial state, his commanders agreed to his wishes of succession.

Babur's sons all became deputies during Babur's life, and he was aware that once he would die, his sons would become each other's rival. To prevent this from happening, he started distributing his territories among the four sons he had. He already installed Kamran, his second son, as the ruler of Kabul in his absence, and Babur wanted Kamran to hold Kabul even after his death. To the eldest son, Humayun, he planned to leave Hindustan. His youngest sons, Hindal and Askari, were to be given territories in Kabul. In his will, Babur directed his sons to respect each other and to support one another, as it was the principle of Central Asian sovereignty.

However, the distrust and rivalry between the brothers were obvious even during Babur's life. When he was ill in 1529, Babur summoned his younger son, Hindal, to his side, but his eldest, Humayun, ordered his brother to stay in Badakhshan and rule instead of him while he visited their ill father. When Babur heard of this, he sent an invitation to Hindal once more, and as the supreme emperor, he overruled Humayun's order. He was very displeased with his eldest son, as he was too willful. But Gulbadan, one of Babur's daughters who wrote the biography of Humayun (*Humayun-Nama*), records her father's fondness for his eldest son. She recalls his love was so great that when Humayun was sick, Babur performed a ritual to transfer the sickness to himself. Humayun recovered while his father began to die. He spent his final days in Agra, which was where he died in 1530. At first, he was buried there, but later, his body was transported to Kabul, which was where he wished to be laid to rest.

Despite Babur's will and the division of his territories, his sons fought for supremacy continuously. Humayun was the successor to the Mughal Empire, but he ultimately proved to be unable to maintain control.

Chapter 3 – Humayun of the Mughal Empire

Humayun, the second emperor
https://en.wikipedia.org/wiki/Humayun#/media/File:Darbar_of_Humayun,_detail,_Humayun._Akbarnama,_1602-4,_British_Library.png

When Babur died in 1530, he was succeeded by his eldest son, Humayun. The young prince was unfamiliar with the lands he inherited, as most of his time was spent outside of India. He had returned to Central Asia after having spent a year fighting his father's wars for conquest in 1526. He only returned to India after he received the news of his father's illness, shortly before he died.

Upon his succession of the Mughal throne, Humayun faced a revolt led by his own brothers. Each of them had their own dynastic ambitions, and they claimed independence from their older brother's rule. Mirza Kamran ruled Kabul, as was his father's wish. However, soon after Babur's death, he expanded his dominion over Kandahar, parts of Central Asia, and Punjab. The main rivalry among brothers was between Humayun and Kamran, while the younger ones, Hindal and Askari, switched their loyalty between them as they pleased. On some occasions, they claimed independence for the regions they controlled. It came to the point where Kamran's forces killed his younger brother Hindal, and an angered Humayun ordered him and Askari to be exiled.

The four brothers also had a cousin, who Babur had adopted as a son, named Mirza Sulaiman. He ruled Badakhshan after Babur's death, and he also accepted the overlordship of Humayun and Kamran, depending on where the political power at the given moment was. He also asserted autonomy for his regions against the will of Babur's sons. While Humayun, Kamran, Hindal, and Askari died fighting each other, Sulaiman outlived them all.

Humayun inherited a large empire, and to effectively control it, he needed to be familiar with the policies and techniques of ruling. Unfortunately, the young prince wasn't. Instead, he sought to install himself as a divine symbol of power, and he organized his court in the image of the cosmic order as it was seen by 16th-century Islam. He thought of himself as the center of the microcosmos that was his court. He was divine, and as such, he wore a veil over his face, sheltering it from the curious courtiers who wanted to bask in his divine splendor. He would occasionally lift his veil and allow his subjects to be dazzled by the light of his image. Personally, he was a follower of the Shattari Sufi mysticism order, which sought to control the cosmic forces through the practice of yoga. It was Humayun who ordered all of his royal tents to be divided into twelve parts, with each part representing one of the zodiac signs. Also, he named the days of the week by celestial bodies and dressed ritually according to what day it was. For example, Tuesday was Mars Day, and he would dress in red robes to symbolically represent the celestial body. Also, he devoted Tuesday to sentencing criminals and war prisoners.

Humayun believed that his imaginative ritualistic rule would persuade his brothers about his supremacy. He divided the administration of the empire according to the natural elements. The military was fire, while the land and building administration was earth. The irrigation of the empire was entrusted to the ministry of water, while his own household was administered by the element of air. Each state official had to wear a robe in the color that belonged to the element of his ministry. The military wore red, land and buildings wore brown robes, the water ministry wore blue, and the royal household was dressed in white. But all of these efforts of symbolism failed to impress his rival brothers, his Central Asian followers, and his new subjects, whether they were Muslim or not. His Central Asian commanders, in particular, resisted his effort to centralize the power in his own persona. They wanted the old ways where they were given positions in the governance, and Humayun had to face repeated uprisings due to his policies.

Early Military Successes

Even though Humayun wasn't familiar with his new Mughal Empire, upon succeeding the throne, he decided to conquer as much of South Asia as possible. He wanted to continue his father's military momentum even though he was surrounded by very rich and powerful rulers and warlords. The Central and Lower Ganges Plains had an ever-shifting coalition of Indo-Afghans and the Sultanate of Bengal. The coalition was supported by local magnates and landowners. Against them, Humayun had some initial victories, but the real threat came from the southwest, where Sultan Bahadur Shah of Gujarat ruled.

Bahadur Shah sought Babur's help when he was fleeing the wrath of his own father and older brother during the dynastic struggle in the Gujarat region. But Babur denied him any help, and he described Bahadur Shah in his writings as a bloodthirsty and audacious man. Nevertheless, Bahadur managed to seize the throne of his father, putting him in charge of the main ports of India, which were crucial for the international trade across the Indian Ocean. Because of this, Bahadur was extremely wealthy, and he used his riches to secure the loyalties of other rulers in the region. He hired and maintained a large army, which he supplied with expensive artillery. He even had Mustafa Rumi Khan as a commander of his artillery forces, one of the gunpowder experts mentioned earlier.

Bahadur Shah was powerful enough to challenge Humayun, and he did so by attacking the Chittor Fort, which defended the point of access to Hindustan. The first attack on the fort was launched in 1533, but it was unsuccessful, and it was followed by a second attack in 1534. Humayun arrived too late to save the fortress, but he decided to invade and conquer his enemy's territory, Gujarat. The armies met at Malwa, where Sultan Bahadur Shah decided to entrench his army behind the fort walls, which were defended by cannons. However, Humayun's forces besieged the fort and starved the army, forcing it to flee. After seeing the defeat, Rumi Khan decided to switch to Humayun's side and join his efforts in conquering Gujarat. Bahadur Shah sought refuge with the governor of Portuguese India, Nuno da Cunha, who resided on the fortified island of Diu. However, Bahadur met his death on the island, as the negotiations with the governor didn't go well. He drowned, but it remains unclear if his death was an assassination or an accident as he was fleeing from the Portuguese.

While Humayun was on his military expedition to conquer the southwestern region of India, a rebellion rose in Hindustan, and his military commanders begged him to return home and deal with the rebels. But Humayun was convinced in his intentions to subdue the rich Gujarat territory, and he did not want to go back to Hindustan. His Central Asian generals then decided to support his younger half-brother, Askari, who was already in Agra, where he had proclaimed himself the sovereign. Humayun was forced to abandon his plans in Gujarat, as he had to secure his power back in Hindustan. He managed to gain his throne back, and he even forgave his younger brother. But the military expenses were high, and since he had abandoned Gujarat, he had nothing to give in reward to his commanders. He needed loot in order to reward his supporters, who already showed how easily their loyalties could be lost. Humayun needed another military expedition urgently, and so, he marched his forces down the Ganges toward Bengal, where Indo-Afghan of the Sur clan, Sher Shah Suri, ruled. He was also known as Sher Khan, "Lion Lord."

Humayun's first major goal was to capture the Chunar fortress in 1537, which was placed in a strategically important geographical location in the region. The fortress was well defended by cannons on its walls, but Humayun's artillery prevailed after the four-month siege. Rumi Khan came up with the idea of placing the cannons on riverboats to bombard the fortress walls directly. They caused so much damage that Sher Shah's son, who commanded the fortress, agreed to negotiations. With the loss of Chunar, Sher Shah was forced to officially submit to the rule of Humayun. Because of his innovative tactics, Rumi Khan received this fortress as a reward. However, he was Indian, and as such, he stood out of the Central Asian circle of Humayun's commanders. He was assassinated by those commanders as soon as he fell into imperial disfavor.

Humayun's forces continued marching over Bengal in search of new treasures and rewards for the military. However, they were unaccustomed to the humidity of this area, and they suffered greatly. Even Humayun gave up the direct command of his forces and chose to close himself in his pleasure palace with his wives and concubines, enjoying opium. The situation back in Hindustan went sour once more when another of Humayun's half-brothers, this time Hindal, proclaimed himself to be the new ruler in Agra. Humayun had to go back and secure his throne once more, but it was the monsoon season, and the roads were impassable. Since Humayun had to delay his return to Hindustan, it created the opportunity for Sher Shah to reorganize his forces and block Humayun's return home.

The Loss of an Empire

It was in June 1539, as Humayun's forces were marching back to Hindustan, that Sher Shah met them once more at Chausa. This time, he had a more effective army, which managed to defeat the Mughal soldiers who were already dispirited by the harsh environment of Bengal. Humayun lost many of his Central Asian commanders, and one of his wives was killed, while the other one was captured. Humayun had to flee, and while crossing the river with his army, he nearly drowned. In his biography, it is recorded that a poor water-carrier named Nizam rescued the emperor. It also says that Nizam was rewarded by being named emperor for a day. However, this act enraged Humayun's commanders and courtiers, and they raised the question of his legitimacy to the throne. If he could transfer the sovereignty so freely, and to a man of low birth no less, what was so divine in him that demanded their respect? This disdain from his commanders continued to deepen as Humayun lost control over some of the Mughal territories. Furthermore, he was constantly challenged by his own brothers, and he had a bad opium habit that led him to resign from active rule from time to time. It is no wonder that Humayun's support was lessening each day.

In 1540, Humayun was resolved to return his lost prestige, and he decided to attack Sher Shah again. However, he lost once more, this time in the Battle of Bilgram on May 17th, 1540. The records note that his army was so demoralized that it scattered even before the main battle began. Humayun, with the help of an Afghan soldier, managed to escape. He decided to lavishly reward this soldier and admit him into the royal household, which created an even deeper divide between him and his commanders. This Afghan soldier,

Shamsuddin Muhammad Atgah Khan, would later become Humayun's son's foster-father. Sher Shah drove Humayun out of Hindustan, and with the loss of the supporters in his own empire, Humayun had to search for refuge in Punjab. After only fourteen years, the Mughal Empire had ended. Sher Shah ruled in place of Humayun, but he did not rule as a Mughal emperor. Instead, he created his own dynasty in northern India, and the territory that was previously known as the Mughal Empire now became the Sur Empire.

Sher Shah ruled for seven years, from 1538 to 1545, and as a leader, he set up a new administration. Even though he ruled the area of Hindustan, Sher Shah chose Sasaram for his capital instead of Agra. Thee economic and military reorganization he implemented under his governance would further be used by the Mughals. Sher Shah contributed to the empire in so many ways that his Mughal successors would come to idolize him. He was the emperor who introduced the first *rupiya*, a silver coin whose name would later become a standard for the currency in the Indian subcontinent. He also organized the first Indian post office. Indeed, Sher Shah's accomplishments during his very short rule would be remembered forever. Even his nemesis Humayun referred to him as "Ustad-I-Badshahan," the teacher of kings.

However, not all was well within Sher Shah's empire. He was accused of leading religious persecutions, and his governance allowed religious violence across the provinces of northern India. He advised his own commanders that they should die during these religious persecutions and wars, for if they died while fighting against the infidels, they would become martyrs. His army oppressed the Hindus of India in particular. One such religious persecution took place at the Kalinjar fort, where every Hindu person—men, women, and children—was put to death. Sher Shah is also known for the destruction of many cities. In order to build a new city, he would destroy the historical site of the previous settlement and then build his city on its ruins. The city of Shergarh is the best example of this practice. This city used to be a site where Hinduism, Buddhism, and Jainism peacefully co-existed. The ruins of the previous settlement provide evidence of a thriving city's existence that preceded Sher Shah's rule.

Humayun the Exile

Humayun was still officially Padshah, and he sought some way to regain his empire. For that, he needed his place of exile to be strategically positioned for the reconquest of Hindustan. His brother Mirza Kamran held Kabul, but he wouldn't allow Humayun and his court passage to the Central Asian homeland. He thought of invading Kashmir, but his commanders were against it. Finally, he contemplated giving up on his empire and becoming a qalandar, a holy man of the Sufi order. In the end, a decision was made to move across the Thar Desert into Sindh, a province of modern Pakistan.

Humayun's court was constantly shrinking, as his Central Asian commanders who served under his father all left him. But he still had some riches, enough to be respected among some of his people but not enough to reward his supporters. In Sindh, some of the landowners were respectful enough to provide his small entourage with food, while others tried to drive him away from their lands. However, Humayun still had the loyalty of a Turkish warrior named Bairam Khan, whose family had been in the service of Babur. With his help and that of his soldiers, Humayun was able to extract enough provisions from those locals who weren't willing to part with their possessions.

According to his biography, which was written by his half-sister Gulbadan, Humayun was attracted to a daughter from a Persian family who was in his entourage. Her name was Hamida Begum, and she was in her early teens. She declined his marriage proposal, thinking she was not worthy of a man of such high status. Her father also objected as Humayun was too poor to marry at that time. But both her and her family eventually were persuaded, and a year after the wedding, in October of 1542, Hamida gave birth to a son named Akbar. A few months later, Humayun's entourage was attacked by his half-brother Askari, and he nearly captured Humayun. But he managed to escape, and together with Hamida and thirty of his faithful followers, he started the long march to Persia. However, his son Akbar was left behind and became his uncle's royal prisoner. A year later, Askari passed Akbar to Kamran, Humayun's brother, who ruled Kabul.

Humayun and his followers marched through mountains and valleys, and in these hostile areas, they were forced to kill their horses in order to eat their meat, which they cooked in soldiers' helmets. Humayun wrote a letter to Shah Tahmasp I of the Safavid dynasty about his coming to Persia. The letter was submissive and handwritten, a gesture that touched the court of Tahmasp so much that they welcomed Humayun and his followers with the greatest of honors. While visiting Persia, Humayun was amazed by its architecture and art, and later, he would employ Persian artists in his own court. The two rulers did not meet for the first six months of Humayun's stay in Persia. But once they did, many lavish parties were organized to celebrate the occasion. There is even a wall painting depicting the meeting of the two monarchs, and it still survives in Chehel Sotoun, Iran.

Shah Tahmasp treated the disgraced Mughal emperor with all the royal honors he could bestow, but he urged Humayun to convert from his Sunni beliefs to Shia Islam, which he accepted. His Mughal followers were reluctant to convert, but eventually, they agreed, as they saw that it was the only way in which Tahmasp would support Humayun's reconquest of the Mughal Empire. After he converted to Shia, Humayun proved to be of true value to Tahmasp. When Kamran offered Kandahar, located in today's Afghanistan, for the exchange of Humayun, Tahmasp refused him. In fact, the Persian ruler was so enraged that Kamran wanted Humayun dead that he prepared a great celebration, in which he announced he was giving Humayun 12,000 cavalrymen to attack Kamran. In return, he wanted to receive Kandahar from Humayun's own hands.

The Restoration of the Mughal Empire

Humayun started his mission to retake his empire in 1545, but it would take him over a decade to succeed. He started slowly by attacking Kandahar, where Askari ruled. With the help of Tahmasp's 12,000 cavalrymen, the city fell after being besieged for four weeks. As promised, he gave the city to Tahmasp, who appointed his infant son as its viceroy. However, the boy soon died, and Humayun thought himself strong enough to confront Tahmasp and rule the city by himself. But after some negotiations, the two monarchs agreed to install a governor who would rule the city under their joint sovereignty.

The same year, Humayun marched his army to take Kabul. Kamran Mirza wasn't loved by his people, and when his soldiers saw Humayun's Persian army approaching, they changed sides, numbering in the hundreds. Kabul was taken over with ease, and Humayun was reunited with his son, Akbar. They organized a large feast in the boy's honor. However, Kamran survived the onslaught, and he built a new army outside the city walls. He would cause Humayun to lose Kabul twice, but each time he did so, Humayun would manage to regain the city once more. Humayun thought of continuing and returning Hindustan under his rule, but he was aware the time wasn't right. Instead, he organized smaller raids, gaining more and more of his homeland territory back, which he would give as a reward to his commanders. This tactic attracted local warlords who offered their bands to Humayun's service. Thus, his army constantly grew.

Humayun suffered constant attacks from his brothers Kamran and Askari, who even captured his son Akbar on a few occasions. Each time he would forgive them until, in 1551, during a raid, they killed Hindal, who was, at the time, the subject of Humayun. To punish his brothers, Humayun exiled them both but not before blinding Kamran. With all of his three brothers out of his way, Humayun could concentrate on recovering Hindustan. He managed to recruit Persians and the younger generation of Central Asian warriors who didn't remember his own failures. In 1555, he took the opportunity of the existing dynastic struggle in the Sur Empire to launch his first attack. Briefly, Sher Shah had died ten years earlier when Humayun wasn't ready to attack. Sher Shah's successor, Islam Shah Suri, died in 1554, creating turmoil and rivalry among his three successors. All three Suri princes marched on Delhi to try and capture it, while the local leaders fought for their independence. The setting was perfect for a Mughal invasion.

Humayun placed his trust in Bairam Khan, a Turkish warlord who was a great tactician, and in February 1555, they captured Lahore and Rohtas Fort. After those conquests, his army took Dipalpur and Jalandhar in Punjab. Moving toward Delhi, where he planned to take the throne, Humayun and Bairam Khan met the Suri army, which numbered 30,000 men. The Mughal army easily defeated their enemy and occupied Sirhind. But Sikandar Shah Suri, one of the Suri pretenders to the throne, gathered an army of 80,000 soldiers and attacked Sirhind on June 22nd, 1555. However, Bairam Khan, the brilliant tactician, imitated the attack Sher Shah Suri had led against Humayun in the Battle of Chausa in 1539, and he defeated the Suri army once more. Humayun's path to Delhi was now open, and he quickly occupied the city, thus reestablishing the Mughal Empire.

Humayun decided to take a different approach to ruling his empire than before. Instead of a centralized state, he opted for the decentralization of the empire. He divided the empire into six semi-autonomous provinces that would be governed by different commanders. Humayun would be the paramount ruler to his new provinces of Delhi, Agra, Kanauj, Jaunpur, Mandu, and Lahore. He moved from province to province with his nomadic court and army, and he would supervise his governors and offer them his personal support when needed. Humayun's young son Akbar was sent to Lahore, where he would learn from Bairam Khan, whose task was to secure Punjab. Kabul was given to his second son, Mirza

Muhammad Hakim, who was still an infant and needed the capable supervision of a trusted guardian.

Seven months after he restored the Mughal Empire, Humayun tripped while going down the steep stairs of his library, seriously injuring himself. Three days later, on January 27th, 1556, Humayun died from his injuries. It is said that Humayun had his arms full of books when he heard the call to prayer while descending the steps of the library. By habit, he bent his knee in a religious bow, but his foot caught his robe, and he tumbled down the steps, hitting his head on the edge of a stone.

Humayun was first buried inside a fort named Purana Quila, but his first wife, Bega Begum, commissioned a grand garden tomb in Delhi to be built in the Mughal style for her husband. This tomb was so grandiose that it set an example for the later Taj Mahal in Agra.

Chapter 4 – The Empire under Emperor Akbar

Akbar the Great

https://en.wikipedia.org/wiki/Akbar#/media/File:Govardhan._Akbar_With_Lion_and_Calf_ca._1630,_Metmuseum_(cropped).jpg

Abu'l-Fath Jalal-ud-din Muhammad Akbar, better known as Akbar the Great, succeeded his father and ruled the Mughal Empire for nearly five decades, from 1556 until 1605. During his rule, the Mughal dynasty rooted itself in Hindustan. Unlike his grandfather and father, Akbar lived in Hindustan most of his life, as did his successors. He was born in Sindh, but he did spend a portion of his childhood in Central Asia as a royal prisoner in Kabul at the court of his uncle Kamran. However, Akbar was very young when his father died, and his accession did not go unchallenged.

To avoid the succession struggles, Humayun's advisors and courtiers held his death as a secret for several weeks. However, their actions did not help the underaged Akbar to strengthen his position as an emperor. He was under the regency of his father's greatest warrior Bairam Khan, and even though Bairam Khan tried to outmaneuver Akbar's rivals and dispatch a force that would defend the borders of the Mughal Empire against the successors of the Sur Empire, his Central Asian commanders didn't agree. In fact, many of them prepared to return to their homeland after Humayun's death.

At this time, back in Central Asia, Kabul was under attack from Prince Mirza Sulaiman, the ruler of Badakhshan. With its problems, Kabul was unable to send help to Hindustan, and the Sur Empire easily reconquered Agra and Delhi. Finally, Bairam Khan persuaded the commanders to give him the main command of the Mughal forces, and they all agreed to march against the Sur usurper Sikandar Shah Suri, who ruled in Punjab. However, he proved to be little more than an annoyance to Akbar's army, and he was easily defeated, thus delivering Delhi back into the fold of the Mughal Empire. However, the real threat to Akbar came from Hemu, a Hindu king who used to serve the Sur Empire as a minister. Under his leadership, the Suri army expelled the Mughals from the Indo-Gangetic Plain in 1556, and Delhi was lost once again.

Before Hemu managed to consolidate his power in the region, Bairam Khan reorganized the Mughal army, and with a thirteen-year-old Akbar, he marched to reclaim Delhi. On November 5th, 1556,

Hemu was defeated, and the Mughal forces occupied Delhi and Agra soon after that. Hemu was captured and executed, and his head was sent to Kabul to be hanged for everyone to see that young Emperor Akbar had won and regained his empire. Even though Hemu's family and supporters were all executed, Akbar erected a minaret in their remembrance and a memorial for Hemu at the spot where he was beheaded.

Emperor Under Regency (1556-1562)

Depiction of the emperor training an elephant

https://en.wikipedia.org/wiki/Akbar#/media/File:Kaiser_Akbar_b%C3%A4ndigt_einen_Elefanten.jpg

For the first four years of his rule, Akbar didn't take an active role in administering his empire. Instead, he enjoyed hunting far away from his court, and he completely relied on his war commander Bairam Khan, who governed as Wakil-us-Sultanat, an agent of the state. After the defeat of Hemu, Bairam Khan's personal control over the governance only grew, and he gained enough power to place his own Central Asian and Iranian people to key official positions.

However, to reward all of his supporters, Bairam Khan needed wealth, and the royal treasuries were quickly emptied. Akbar was seen as a weak ruler because of his young age, and to exploit this Mughal weakness, the Persian Safavids, in 1557, wrestled full control over Kandahar from the Mughals. However, Bairam Khan managed to expand the empire in 1558 when he conquered Ajmer, Jaunpur, and Gwalior.

The emperor enjoyed his hunts, and later in life, he would often combine his military expeditions with hunting. While he was young, he hunted not just for pleasure but also for the practice of martial skills and for gaining influence and reputation among his subordinates. He especially enjoyed *gamarha*, a Mongol-style of hunting in which hundreds or even thousands of horsemen took part. This style of hunting demanded very good organizational and leadership skills in order to perform it with success. Another one of Akbar's pleasures was capturing wild elephants and taming them for battle. In India, elephants were seen as symbols of sovereignty, and it was seen as a special honor to ride this animal into battle. Akbar risked his life very often in his youth just because he wanted to capture, tame, and train his own elephants.

During the period of regency, Akbar devoted time to meet Hindu leaders, and unlike his predecessors, he valued Hindu advice. He didn't rely only on Central Asian and Iranian Muslim commanders. Because of this, many Hindu Rajputs, members of a warrior caste of India, valued Akbar and saw a potential ally in him. They joined the Mughal army, and because they were so well accepted in the Mughal court, they saw it as an opportunity to gather resources and wealth. Later, when Akbar took over the governance of his empire, he would place some of the most loyal Hindu Rajputs into his own household. Among the first Rajputs he met was Bihari Mal, who became the emperor's good friend and whose daughter Akbar would later marry.

Toward Bairam Khan, Akbar was always affectionate, and he treated him with the utmost respect and love as an adoptive father. He even referred to him as Khan Baba, "Noble Father." However, other commanders and courtiers sought to undermine the relationship Akbar had with Bairam Khan. They challenged Bairam's authority and wanted to replace him. Thus, they competed for Akbar's affection throughout his teenage years. There were two main clans that opposed Bairam Khan's authority. One was led by Shamsuddin Muhammad Atgah Khan, better known simply as Ataga Khan, an Afghan soldier who was rewarded with a high position in the Mughal court for saving Humayun's life back in 1540. It was Ataga Khan's wife who was the wet nurse and foster-mother of Akbar, which would make Ataga the emperor's foster-father. Ataga Khan's family remained with Akbar when his parents had to abandon him. They were even with him in the court of Kabul, where Akbar was a royal hostage. It was only natural that Akbar had respect and affection for this family too.

Another faction that opposed Bairam Khan was centered around Akbar's second wet nurse and foster-mother Maham Anga. Together with her relatives, she accused Bairam Khan of arrogance, and she would often cast speculations on Bairam's actions to diminish his prestige. However, Bairam was too proud and often harsh when responding to Maham Anga's accusations, and it led to tensions between him and the young emperor. Throughout his youth, Akbar had no control over the royal treasury, meaning he had no personal wealth to speak of, and it was difficult for him to move against Bairam Khan, who enjoyed all the luxuries of the palace. Once he was challenged, Bairam Khan was ruthless, and he demanded his opposition to beg him for forgiveness. However, Akbar did not approve of such behavior, and he issued a royal decree against Bairam in 1560. Bairam Khan lost many of his supporters, as they saw the decree as a sign of his disgrace and instead joined Akbar. The regent had no other choice than to surrender the symbols of his rank. However, Akbar still loved his Khan Baba, and he gave him a choice: he could stay at his court as an advisor, or he could go to Mecca on a pilgrimage. Bairam chose to go on a pilgrimage, and Akbar assigned him some land properties as his well-deserved pension once he returned from Mecca. However, Bairam Khan never returned to Hindustan again. He also never reached Mecca. He was assassinated in Sindh by a hostile Afghan who retaliated for the death of Hemu.

Even though the clans successfully disposed of Bairam Khan, they continued the struggle over the influence on Akbar's rule. Maham Anga was very successful at dictating politics once she gave her support to Munim Khan, who became the official Vizier (the emperor's advisor and minister of the empire). Munim Khan was an old favorite courtier of Akbar's father, and he helped Maham Anga to promote her son, Adham Khan, in the court. It was during this period, in 1562, to be specific, that the Mughals conquered Malwa from the Rajputs. Also, the Chunar fortress was taken over, which had previously been held by the Indo-Afghans who constantly rebelled. This was when the clash between Adham Khan and Akbar happened, as Anga's son killed the captured women of Chunar instead of sending them to Akbar. He also ordered the assassination of Ataga Khan, his opposer, to gain even more influence and power in the royal court.

The consequence of the clash between Akbar and Adham Khan was that the emperor finally asserted his power, making his courtiers who hungered for power flee the court. Those who constantly schemed and pushed their agendas forward were punished, and Akbar finally started his independent rule, free of regents and power-hungry advisors. Learning his lesson, Akbar did not allow any of his officials to gather too much power. All the authority Bairam Khan once had Akbar divided among his ministers, and now they had to work under the emperor's direct supervision. It is unknown how much power and influence the women of Akbar's court had, but he often listened to the advice of his family members who had no high-ranking status.

It is believed that Akbar suffered dyslexia, as he was illiterate, which was very strange for a person of his rank. But it is recorded that he had an extraordinary memory. He would store all the documents and reports that were read to him in his memory and surprise his officials with the knowledge of the details of outdated documents. He took it upon himself to personally issue every order, promotion, demotion, award, and appointment to his high-ranking officials, commanders, ministers, and courtiers. He also personally took care of many royal marriages, which helped him to create a vast network of new supporters. Akbar also actively took part in planning military strategies and leading his own army. Additionally, Akbar is credited with the invention of many new weapons; however, this could just be an exaggeration from the imperial chroniclers. He made sure to keep up to date with important events by employing news writers who would gather all the important information from all the ministries, the whole empire in general, and even neighboring rulers. And not only did he oversee the people in his kingdom, but he also personally supervised his rich imperial stables, which housed horses, camels, and elephants.

Administration and the Army

Akbar dedicated his rule to the expansion of his empire. As a military empire, the Mughals needed a vast, ever-growing army and an administration that would provide for such an empire. They had to exact tribute and revenues from all the areas they continuously conquered, as the empire demanded a large income to support its army, administration, and Akbar's court. Akbar's predecessors, both Babur and Humayun, seized the treasures of the territories they conquered and also forced the local rulers and landowners to find as many sources of revenue as possible from their territories and give them to the emperor as a tribute. Then the emperor would divide the profits among his loyal commanders to reward them.

Akbar had trouble with many of the local rulers, as they would not comply with his administration. Eventually, he replaced them with those who were more compliant, or their territories would simply be taken and directed by Akbar's administration instead. By doing this, Akbar secured local rulers, Rajputs, and landowners who would give him and his family full support in exchange for protection and the opportunity to rise in political power. Uncultivated lands were granted to prominent people who would turn it into productive lands, who would only start paying tribute to the emperor after they got them up and running. However, the Mughal Empire never established a monopoly over Indian military labor or made a habit of using coercion, and because of it, they often suffered rebellions. During the reign of Akbar, there were 144 rebellions recorded, which were mostly led by local landowners who were free to hire soldiers as they wished.

Although Akbar's predecessors practiced predatory tribute extortion, he was different. Akbar opted for a more centralized model that would exact revenues but be strictly controlled by a set of rules and records, which would supervise both the payers and collectors. He also recruited among the Hindu to fill the new offices of the local administration. Since they were locals, they already possessed the knowledge and experience required for managing the land, and they already had the trust of the local landowners.

Akbar, together with Bairam Khan, modeled his administration on the one used by Sher Shah Suri during his reign of northern India. However, while Bairam Khan spent the gathered revenues to gain supporters, Akbar invested in further modernization and innovation of the administrative and bureaucratic systems. In 1566, Akbar implemented a system of fixed taxes, which were based on the productivity of a territory. But this was extremely hard on the peasants, as the tax rate was fixed according to the imperial court where wealthy people who were able to pay high revenues lived.

Akbar had to decentralize the system and assess a territory's revenue annually, which opened the door for corruption. In 1580, Akbar replaced this system with one called Dahsala, in which revenue was calculated as one-third of the average production of the past ten years. This revenue had to be paid to the emperor in money instead of produce. It was far from a perfect system, but it showed the best results. It needed refining due to the corruption present, and much was done to help fight this corruption and make it possible for both peasants and landowners to prosper. Akbar's administration grouped the areas that produced a similar amount of revenue into a number of assessment groups for easier management, and the local prices were taken into account in order not to agitate the locals who worked the land. If the harvest was destroyed by a flood or drought, the peasants of those affected areas were freed from paying the taxes for that year. The Dahsala system was invented by Raja Todar Mal, a finance minister who worked under both Sher Shah Suri and Akbar. By 1583, the administration and the taxation system were fully implemented throughout the empire.

The landowners of the empire were known as zamindars, and they had the hereditary right to collect and share the produce of their lands, but in turn, they were obliged to provide loans and to improve the agriculture of their regions. They were considered nobles, and they had the right to pass their aristocratic title to their offspring. The zamindars commanded their own army, and since they were often unsatisfied by the Mughal Empire's administration, they would lead rebellions against Emperor Akbar. During the Mughal Empire, all local rulers and Indian princes were called zamindars, whether their titles were actually rai, raja, rana, rao, or rawat. In the Persian world, they were all called zamindars, and the contemporary historian of Akbar's time, Arif Qandhari, figured there were around 300 such rulers under the overlordship of Akbar.

In the army, Akbar implemented a system of ranking for all his high-ranking officers, known as the Mughal mansabdari system. Four centuries earlier, a similar system was used by Akbar's ancestor Genghis Khan, and one had also been used more recently by Sher Shah Suri. Akbar further developed the old system, making it far more sophisticated. This system was implemented in about 1574 when Akbar assigned a numerical grade from 10 to 5,000 to each of his top thousand officers. However, only 33 numerical values were used, each bringing its officer a specific salary.

In turn, the officers had to provide a specific number of cavalry or any other type of soldier, with the number depending on their rank, and they also had to pay for recruited men from their own pockets. Those who ranked with a score of 500 and above were emir, also spelled as amir (noblemen). The system assured every officer that they could move through the ranks during their career and rank higher by performing their duties better.

In the Mughal Empire, the military officers were also given administrative tasks, as the commanders were appointed as governors of newly conquered areas as well. These ranks were not passed down to their successors. An officer could succeed a governor, but he would remain of a lower score until he proved himself more. An office didn't have a specific score, and it would not have been feasible for it to have one, as Akbar often recalled his commanders and appointed new ones. He would suddenly decide to transfer one governor to some other province and assign him to a different administrative office.

The mansab, the grade of an official, wasn't a hereditary system. A father couldn't transfer his mansab to his children, but one's birth did influence the initial ranking of a person. After all, it was by birthright that one would be set on the career path of a commander. Sons always started at a lower rank than their fathers, and they had to prove themselves through hard administrative work and military achievements. But not all new recruits started with the same score. Sons of more prominent officers would start with a higher mansab than those of common soldiers. The princes usually held the highest mansab, scoring higher than anyone else. However, they were not all equal. Their value depended on much more than the score since age, one's family, and the emperor's personal opinion of them made all the difference. The leaders of the newly conquered lands were also given very high initial ranks, as they were kept in their princely positions.

The property of all mansabdars, the soldiers who served under the mansab system, was inherited by the emperor after their death. There would be no inheritance left for the family of the deceased officer, and because of this, mansabdars never built lavish palaces.

Instead, they invested their salaries in building temples, mosques, or their own tombs, as these could not be taken by the emperor. However, if Akbar had a favorite among them, he would often give the land and his properties to his family after the officer died. Mansabdars also invested in education, particularly in administrative skills, as well as in his supporters and followers, as these could be passed to his offspring while the land, salary, and household could not.

Akbar's Expansion of the Empire

Akbar started the expansion of his empire when he was only eighteen. He prepared his army to take the southern territories of the Indian subcontinent, namely Rajputana and Malwa, but in 1559, the dispute he had with Bairam Khan put a hold on this military campaign. Once he dismissed Bairam Khan in 1560, Akbar resumed his idea of conquering the south. First came the conquest of Malwa. The conquest was led by Akbar's foster-brother Adham Khan and a commander named Pir Muhammad Khan. Akbar had a claim to this province, as it was part of the Mughal Empire before his father lost it to Sher Shah Suri.

Malwa was ruled by Sultan Baz Bahadur, whose army was defeated by the Mughals in 1561 in the Battle of Sarangpur. In fact, the Afghan forces of Baz Bahadur deserted once they saw the power of the Mughal army when they occupied their capital of Mandu. There, the Mughals massacred the citizens and seized the royal treasury and harem. Akbar even had to intervene and dispose of the bloodthirsty Adham Khan, who, even though he became the governor of the province after the conquest, continued being cruel toward the locals. Baz Bahadur fled to Khandesh, but he was pursued by Pir Muhammad Khan, who was killed after finding himself in the midst of a military clash between two of the Deccan sultanates. This conflict briefly returned Malwa to the rule of Baz Bahadur, but the Mughals returned in 1562 to conquer it once more.

Abdullah Khan Uzbeg was the commander of the renewed conquest of Malwa, but Baz Bahadur managed to escape again. He found refuge in the Gondwana hills, and in 1568, he found shelter at the court of Udai Singh II, the ruler of Mewar. However, Baz Bahadur managed to negotiate his position with the Mughal emperor, and once he surrendered in 1570, he was given a mansab of 2,000 and a position among the Mughal noblemen.

With Malwa now under his control, Akbar was one step closer toward regaining all of the Hindustan territories of his ancestors. However, there was still another northern Indian province that needed to be dealt with in order for Akbar to achieve this victory. Garha was a hilly area in central India; it was sparsely populated and did not have much to offer except a large herd of wild elephants, which was a priceless prize for the Mughal emperor. This province fell in 1564 after its warrior queen, Rana Durgavati, committed suicide when her army was defeated at the Battle of Damoh. With this province, the Mughal Empire was secured, and the whole north of India was once more under the rule of the Mughals.

With all the territories secured, Akbar focused on expanding his kingdom, and the first to suffer an attack was Rajputana. The Mughals already ruled some of the territories of Rajputana, such as Mewat and Ajmer. However, it was time for Abkar to further spread his influence in the heartland of Rajputana, where no other ruler dared to go. He started this conquest in 1561, and most of the territories accepted Akbar's supremacy without much conflict. However, Mewar and Marwar remained unconquered. The leaders of these territories, Udai Singh II and Chandrasen Rathore, respectively, continued to defy Akbar. Udai Singh, as the head of the Sisodia clan, possessed the highest status among the Indian kings, and he was also the descendant of Rana Sanga, who had fought Babur in 1527. Thus, it was imperative for Akbar to make this Indian ruler submit to his authority.

The capital of Mewar was the fortress city of Chittor, and it was a strategically important location because it laid on the shortest route to Gujarat. This means that whoever held Chittor would essentially hold the key to the heartland of Rajputana. When the Mughals attacked,

Udai Singh retreated from his court to the hills of Mewar, and he left his capital to be defended by two warriors. In February 1568, the Chittor Fort fell but not before it sustained damage under the four-month-long siege. Akbar beheaded all of the surviving soldiers of Mewar, as well as 30,000 citizens, and displayed their heads on the city towers. This was a common practice during wartime, as the conqueror needed to show off his authority. Udai Singh II's power was completely broken, and he never left his mountain retreat. Akbar didn't bother to pursue him; instead, he left him be.

The next to fall was Rajputana, one of the most powerful fortresses in the subcontinent. In 1568, it fell, but not before its soldiers endured several months of siege. With the taking of Ranthambore, Rajputana was now under Akbar's rule, and most of the kings of these territories submitted to him. Only some clans in Mewar continued to resist, but they were easily dealt with. Once Udai Singh's son Pratap Singh I succeeded his father, he tried to resist Akbar but was defeated at the Battle of Haldighati in 1576. To celebrate the complete submission of Mewar, Akbar rose a new capital city near Agra named it Fatehpur Sikri, "the city of victory." However, Pratap Singh, who survived the battle, continued to rebel against the Mughals. He actually managed to regain most of his father's kingdom while Akbar was still alive.

The next objectives for the Mughal emperor were the territories of Gujarat and Bengal. Both of these territories connected India with Asia, Africa, and Europe, and as such, they were of paramount importance to the trade in India. With the conquest of these territories, Akbar would get rid of the rebelling Mughal nobles who had found refuge in Gujarat, as well as the Afghans under their ruler Sulaiman Khan Karrani in Bengal.

With Rajputana and Malwa now under Akbar's rule, Gujarat was the next to be attacked, as it was surrounded by Mughal territories. Besides having the busiest seaport and being a major trading center in India, Gujarat had fertile and productive lands in its heartland and a well-established textile industry that brought considerable riches to its leaders. Although this was a good reason to conquer this seaside state, Akbar's main motivation was in the fact that in the south of Gujarat was a haven for his Mughal political enemies, who led their rebellions and continued to scheme against him from their bases there. In 1572, Akbar occupied Ahmedabad and other northern cities of Gujarat. When Ahmedabad, the capital of Gujarat, fell, Akbar was proclaimed the official sovereign of the province. His political enemies continued to resist, though, but the emperor managed to drive them out of Gujarat in 1573. All of the coastal cities, including the commercial capital Surat, capitulated to Akbar. Muzaffar Shah III, the king of Gujarat, hid in a cornfield; after he was found, instead of disposing of him, Akbar gave him a small allowance so he could retire.

After dealing with Gujarat, Akbar was free to turn his focus on Bengal, the last territory under Afghan control. Bengal was ruled by Sulaiman Khan Karrani, who had been a war chieftain under Sher Shah Suri when Humayun was defeated. Sulaiman Khan wanted to avoid any conflict with Akbar and managed to stay independent through diplomatic efforts, but his son, Daud Khan, decided to go on the offensive once he succeeded the Bengal throne in 1572. Sulaiman Khan acknowledged Akbar's supremacy to some extent, which brought peace to his lands. Daud Khan, on the other hand, publicly proclaimed his defiance to Akbar. The Mughal governor of Bihar, a province located next to Bengal, was ordered to deal with Daud Khan, but Akbar felt challenged, and so, he eventually set out to deal with Bengal in person.

Patna, the capital of Bihar, was seized in 1574, and instead of continuing to Bengal, Akbar instructed his generals to carry on the conquest while he returned to Fatehpur Sikri, the new capital. At the Battle of Tukaroi in 1575, the Mughal army won a decisive victory, and Bengal was annexed, as well as the parts of Bihar that were still under the rule of Daud Khan. However, Akbar left the territory of Orrisa as a fief to the Karrani dynasty. Daud Khan rebelled again a year later, though, and he attempted to retrieve the entirety of

Bengal, but he didn't have a large base of supporters. However, after his rebellion was defeated, he was forced to flee into exile. Akbar ordered his capture, and soon Daud Khan's head was sent to the emperor.

Military Campaigns in Afghanistan and Central Asia

After the conquest of Bengal and Gujarat, Akbar was occupied with the administrative and military improvement of his empire. It wasn't until 1581 that he organized a big military campaign, though there were always enough rebellions to quell in the meantime, and he found ways to keep his army busy. Mirza Muhammad Hakim, the emperor's brother, invaded Punjab in 1581, but Akbar easily expelled him from the Hindustan territories. However, he didn't think that defeating his brother once was enough, so Akbar continued to pursue Hakim all the way to Kabul, as he wanted to end the threat his brother represented to the Mughal Empire, once and for all.

Akbar had trouble persuading his commanders to leave India and fight a far-off war. Babur once had the problem of persuading his comrades to inhabit India, and now, their descendants didn't want to leave. It was especially hard to persuade the Hindu commanders, as they were forbidden to cross the Indus River due to their traditional beliefs. Hindus of high castes are prohibited, by a religious taboo, from crossing water surfaces as it is believed that by doing so, they will lose their honor and social respect, and thus, they will lose their caste. In the Mughal period, this taboo included rivers, but later it became restricted to only sea voyages. The taboo is known either as kala pani, which literally translates to "black water," or as Samudrolanghana. This taboo still exists in Hinduism, but there are certain rituals one can perform to recover his lost caste after he crosses the water's surface.

To convince his officers, Akbar paid their salaries eight months in advance, which was enough to spur them on. In August, Akbar conquered Kabul, and his brother fled to the mountains. However, Akbar only stayed in Kabul for three weeks. Kabul was then left in the hands of the emperor's sister, Bakht-un-Nisa Begum, while he returned to India. Hakim returned to Kabul after Akbar pardoned him, and he received a high position as an administrative officer. When Muhammad Hakim died in 1585 due to health issues caused by alcoholism, Akbar took Kabul under his direct rule and made it a province of the Mughal Empire.

Akbar moved his capital to Lahore, in the north, in order to be closer to the troublesome areas of his empire. The Uzbeks, now led by Abdullah Khan Shaybanid, continued to be the main threat of the Mughals. Stationed beyond the Khyber Pass, they harassed the borders of the Mughal Empire, but they weren't the only ones. Some Afghan tribes who occupied the border territories often caused unrest in the area, as they were inspired by their new religious leader, Bayazid Pir Roshan, who founded the Roshaniyya movement to fight against social injustice in the Mughal Empire. Roshan and his followers believed in egalitarianism, or what we would call today communist social systems. To keep Akbar occupied and away from their territories, the Uzbeks paid the Afghans to stir up the situation on their border.

However, there was no major conflict between the Mughals and the Uzbeks, as Akbar managed to negotiate a pact with Abdullah Khan. During this period, the Safavid dynasty held the Khorasan region, in today's Iran, and the Uzbeks wanted to invade the area. In order to do so, they needed the Mughals to not meddle with them. In return, Abdullah Khan promised the Uzbeks would stop supporting the Afghans and would stop offering them refuge from the Mughal Empire. Akbar was ready to deal with the Afghans, and the first attack against them was led by commanders Zain Khan and Raja Birbal. However, their campaign was a disaster, and while retreating over the mountainous area of the Malandarai Pass in 1586, Birbal was killed. Akbar did not wait, and he immediately dispatched another army to contain the Yusufzai, an Afghan tribe, in the mountains. For the next six years, the Mughals were successful in bringing many Afghan war chiefs under their rule.

Akbar still continued to dream about the conquest of Central Asia, especially the territories that make up today's Afghanistan. However, some parts of those territories, such as Badakhshan and Balkh, were under Uzbek rule, and the Mughal emperor wasn't in any haste to break the deal he had made with them. During the 17th century, Akbar's grandson would actually occupy these territories, albeit briefly. Even though his dream of a unified Central Asia wasn't accomplished, Akbar managed to achieve a lot in the territories of the northern frontiers. When Abdullah Khan of the Uzbeks died in 1598, the Mughal rule over the territories of the Afghan tribes was secured, as the threat of the Uzbeks breaking their end of the deal passed. By 1600, the last rebellious Afghan tribe was subdued, and the Roshaniyya movement had been suppressed. All of the prominent people of this movement were exiled, and the son of Roshan, Jalaluddin, was killed in 1601.

During his stay in Lahore in 1586, Akbar dispatched an army to conquer Kashmir in the Upper Indus Basin. Previously, Akbar requested that the ruler of Kashmir, Ali Shah, submit to the Mughal Empire and send his son to be a royal hostage in Akbar's court. When Ali Shah refused, the Mughal emperor saw the opportunity to attack. However, no major conflict happened as Ali Shah surrendered immediately. However, his second son Yaqub raised a rebellion against the Mughals and proclaimed himself king. He resisted submitting to the Mughal emperor for the next three years. Akbar was forced to move from Lahore and deal with this rebellion personally. In June 1589, Yaqub surrendered, and the rebellion ended. The next to fall was the Sindh territory in the Lower Indus Valley. After the Battle of Sehwan in 1591, where the outnumbered Mughals brought defeat to the army of Jani Beg, the ruler of Thatta in southern Sindh, the Mughals had firm control of the whole Indus Valley area.

Akbar also led military campaigns against the Safavid dynasty in Kandahar and the Deccan sultans. The Deccan sultanates were five kingdoms occupying the territories of the Deccan Plateau:

Ahmednagar, Berar, Bidar, Bijapur, and Golconda. They all eventually submitted to Akbar after they were defeated by the superior Mughal army. Kandahar was conquered in 1595, and the Deccan sultans were defeated by 1601. Akbar was so successful in his expansion of the Mughal Empire that by 1605, he ruled a large swath of territory, extending from the Bay of Bengal to Kandahar and Badakhshan. His territories bordered the western sea in Sindh, and from there, his influence spread well into central India.

Chapter 5 – One Hundred Years of the Mughal Empire (1605–1707)

Akbar died on October 27th, 1605. He had been suffering from dysentery since October 3rd and was unable to recover. After his death, Akbar was buried in Sikandra, Agra, in a tomb that was an architectural marvel at the time.

The Mughal Empire he left was a secular empire that wanted to emphasize cultural integration. In India, Akbar is praised as a powerful leader who did not rely only on his military power but also on diplomacy. However, in Pakistan, he is often forgotten and not even mentioned as it is believed he weakened Islam with his religious tolerance. Akbar not only accepted Hinduism as the rightful religion of his empire, but he also invited two Christian Jesuits to preach Christianity. However, once they started condemning Islam and speaking against the prophet Muhammad, they were forced to leave the empire.

Akbar was succeeded by his son, Nur-ud-din Muhammad Salim. He wasn't the eldest son, but he was the only surviving one, as the others had died during their infancy. Salim Mirza was known to enjoy earthly pleasures, such as alcohol and his harem. He had twenty wives while he was still a prince and numerous concubines. He was persuaded by his advisors to rebel against Emperor Akbar, and he led an army to start a civil war right before Akbar's death. However, when Akbar fell ill, Salim Mirza made peace with his father. Salim was also known for his cruelty as he liked to torture his enemies. He was a disobedient son, and Akbar tried to reform him and prepare him for the succession. However, Akbar started favoring his grandson, Khusrau Mirza, instead. He even voiced the idea of making Khusrau his successor and renouncing Salim. However, Akbar had no time to make his will as he suddenly fell ill and soon died.

Jahangir (r. 1605-1627)

Portrayal of Jahangir

https://en.wikipedia.org/wiki/Jahangir#/media/File:Indian_-_Single_Leaf_of_a_Portrait_of_the_Emperor_Jahangir_-_Walters_W705_-_Detail.jpg

In September 1605, Salim Mirza was crowned the Mughal emperor, and he took the name Jahangir, the "World-Conqueror." Khusrau Mirza challenged his father's succession, stating that he was Akbar's choice, but his father imprisoned him in the fort of Agra. As a punishment, Jahangir blinded his son by piercing his eyes with wires. Some sources say the Mughal emperor continued to be cruel toward his first son, saying that he would bring Khusrau in chains wherever he traveled. Jahangir expected his son to appear before him each day and offer his respect, but Khusrau continued to defy him. Finally, he gave the prince to his younger son, Khurram Mirza, who killed Khusrau in order to clear his own path to succession.

As an emperor, Jahangir was determined to rise above his predecessors. He improved his father's imperial model, but he also strived to centralize the government around himself, as he thought of an emperor as a holy figure, closer to the divine than his subjects. When Jahangir rose to the throne of the Mughal Empire, he inherited the treasures that came with it, and he used these riches to gain new supporters by raising their salaries and rewarding the officials who pleased him.

To show off his power, Jahangir issued new coins, increasing their size by 20 percent. However, this decision proved to be destructive for the economy of the Mughal Empire, and after only six years, Jahangir returned to the old standard size of the coins. Although his ideas were not always successful, Jahangir continued to innovate coinage. He was proud of his idea to decorate the coins with a zodiac sign for the month of its production. Some coins had his own portrait, complete with a wine glass, and it was these coins that offended many orthodox Muslims, who were against alcohol consumption. Although Jahangir was a renowned consumer of both alcohol and drugs, which led him to suffer serious health issues, he would often ban the production of both under the excuse of religious piety.

Just as his predecessor Babur had, Jahangir kept a personal journal in which he detailed his daily life. Because he never had his journal revised, we are left with the evidence of all of the emperor's thoughts, mood swings, and attitudes. He described his opium and alcohol addiction, as well as the health consequences they left on him. By the age of 26, Jahangir's hands shook so badly that he had to be fed by his attendees. Even a cup of tea had to be brought to his mouth. He got to the point where he had to consume the drug in order to be able to function.

In his journal, Jahangir also described the business of the Mughal Empire, especially trade. The Portuguese were already established on the west coast of the Indian subcontinent, and together with the British East India Company, and later with the Dutch East India Company, they increased the economy of the Mughal Empire with foreign trade. There was a high demand for Indian textiles and other products in Europe, and they were spending their silver from the Americas on buying and investing in Indian production. In return, crops from America entered India, such as maize and tobacco, which were then grown in the fields of the Mughal Empire. Although Emperor Akbar didn't believe in the health benefits of tobacco, it was actually Jahangir who banned its consumption at his court, claiming that it brought a disturbance in people's temperaments and constitutions.

Though he launched a few military campaigns, Jahangir never engaged in the wars personally. Instead, he enjoyed traveling the empire and admiring the beauty of its nature and art. Although some contemporary scholars accused him of cowardice, it wasn't necessarily essential for the emperor to be present on the battlefield in order for the campaign to be successful. In fact, modern historians think his absence from the battlefield is a display of the stability in the Mughal Empire. Jahangir continued to expand the empire throughout his reign, and his armies were all victorious on the northern, western, and eastern borders. However, he failed to completely integrate the newly conquered territories, which would later lead to the weakening of the empire.

In 1594, while he was still just a prince, Akbar sent Jahangir to deal with the Sisodia Rajputs of Mewar, who continued to defy the Mughal Empire. But Jahangir had little success then, and once he became the emperor, he sent his second son, Parviz, to end the campaign. Parviz also failed, and it was Jahangir's third son, Khurram, who finally negotiated the submission of the ruler of

Mewar, Rana Amar Singh I, on February 5th, 1615. Rana Amar Singh was the most powerful of the Rajput leaders at the time, and it was essential for the Mughal Empire to show its dominance over Mewar. The Rajput leader was hard to break, though, and the whole Mughal court had to be moved to Ajmer from 1613 to 1616 in order to support the campaign against Mewar. In 1616, the Mughals won against the rebels of the Deccan frontier. Even though Parviz Mirza had previously conquered the city of Ahmednagar in 1605, the area continued to be affected by the stubborn rebellions against the Mughal Empire.

Jahangir died in 1627 after he had suffered a severe cold during his journey from Kabul to Kashmir. As he was so far away from Lahore, where he had commissioned his tomb to be built, his entrails were taken out in order to preserve the body, and they were buried at Baghsar Fort in Kashmir. His body was then sent to be buried in Shahdara Bagh, a suburb of Lahore. Jahangir is widely perceived as a weak and incapable ruler. Scholars see him as a man that was not fit to be an emperor, and they all agree he would have been a happier man if he was left to deal with the arts and nature, as those remained his passions throughout his life. Jahangir had a habit of retreating to his private life in order to avoid his duties as an emperor. Although he wished to be better than all of his predecessors, he couldn't keep up with a life that wasn't suitable for him. To compensate for his dissatisfaction, he indulged in opium and wine, which only brought even more laziness and apathy for his empire.

Shah Jahan (r. 1628-1658)

Shah Jahan, the fifth Mughal emperor
https://en.wikipedia.org/wiki/Shah_Jahan#/media/File:'Jujhar_Singh_Bundela_Kneels_in_Submission_to_Shah_Jahan',_painted_by_Bichitr,_c._1630,_Chester_Beatty_Library_(cropped).jpg

Even before the death of Emperor Jahangir, his third son, Shahab-ud-din Muhammad Khurram (mentioned above as Khurram Mirza), rebelled. Jahangir married a widowed daughter of a Persian noble, Nur Jahan, in 1611. She became an extremely influential person in the court, and thus, the young prince resented her. She married her daughter from her first marriage to Shahzada Shahryar, Khurram's youngest brother, and then used her influence to promote him as the next emperor. Enraged, Khurram Mirza raised an army in 1622 and started a rebellion against his father, who had fallen under the spell of his scheming wife, Nur Jahan.

However, in March of 1623, the young prince was defeated, and he had to seek refuge in Mewar, where Maharaja Karan Singh II took him in. Even though his rebellion wasn't successful, and he ultimately had to submit to his father, Khurram continued to resent his stepmother, and the tension between the two continued to grow. Since the inheritance of the Mughal Empire was not regulated by the law of primogeniture, the princes had to earn the inheritance of the throne through their military successes and through the power and influence they had in the court. This means that rebellions and civil wars were common in the empire.

Even though Nur Jahan used her influence to install her own brother, Asaf Khan, as the vizier, once Jahangir died, her plans of succession were unfruitful. Asaf Khan was a supporter of Khurram, and he ensured his sister's confinement once the emperor was dead. Asaf Khan also expertly managed all the court intrigues to assure the accession of Khurram Mirza, who took the regnal name Shah Jahan, "King of the World." The first action of the new emperor was to put to death everyone who opposed him and to place his stepmother under arrest. To secure his position as emperor, Shah Jahan executed his half-brother Shahryar, his nephews Dawar and Garshasp, and the sons of his older brother, Khusrau Mirza, who had been executed much earlier. Even though the sons of the late prince Daniyal Mirza, who died due to complications of alcoholism, did not oppose him directly, Shah Jahan decided to kill them nonetheless so he could rule the empire free of any threats.

Shah Jahan inherited his father's almost empty royal treasury, but he was determined to show off his power and the stability of his empire through lavish ceremonies, artwork, and architecture. He constructed a magnificent throne, known as the Peacock Throne, which was lavishly decorated with various gems and gold. It took him seven years to gather all the needed precious stones for the throne. Shah Jahan also invested heavily in architecture. Even though many magnificent structures of Mughal architecture were built on his orders, the most magnificent is still considered to be the Taj Mahal, located in the city of Agra. It was commissioned in 1632, and it was intended to be a tomb for his favorite wife, Mumtaz Mahal. The stories of their love still fill the pages of Indian literature. The Taj

Mahal also serves as his own tomb, as he requested to be buried next to his favorite wife.

To finance all of his architectural projects, Shah Jahan lowered the base salary of his mansabdars, even if they were of higher ranks. This decision would lead to political instability later in his rule. However, the military of the Mughal Empire remained strong. The various sources from 1648 state that the army of Shah Jahan consisted of 911,400 infantry, musketeers, and artillery soldiers and of 185,000 sowars, a Mughal title for cavalry units. It was Shah Jahan who introduced the Marwari horses into the army, as they were his favorite breed. He also commissioned the mass production of cannons, making his empire a military machine. To be able to supply such a huge army, he had to increase the taxes he demanded from his citizens. And even though his economic decisions had a huge impact on the later years of his rule, the Mughal Empire was generally very stable.

Shah Jahan continued the steady expansion of the empire that his father had previously initiated. His own sons led military campaigns, especially to the north and west. The emperor also annexed the kingdoms of Baglana, Mewar, and Bundelkhand. In the territories of the Deccan sultanates, Shah Jahan captured Daulatabad Fort in 1632. Other Deccan sultanates soon followed: Golconda submitted to Shah Jahan in 1635, and Bijapur did so the next year. Shah Jahan appointed his son, Aurangzeb, as the viceroy of the Deccan, and Aurangzeb would later go on to conquer the rebelling Baglana, Golconda, and Bijapur in 1656 and 1657.

Shah Jahan knew, from his own experience, that once the time came, the succession wars between his sons would start. He wanted to prolong the period of peace for as long as he could and postpone the succession drama until after his death. He had four sons, and even though he favored his eldest, Dara Shikoh, he wanted to protect his other sons. Dara was kept close to the court, as his father felt the need to personally prepare him for the rule. He awarded his eldest with various dignities and titles, which demonstrated to others that he was the heir apparent. Both Dara and the emperor's favorite daughter, Jahanara, were children of his first and favorite wife, Mumtaz Mahal. The siblings were very close, and Jahanara openly supported her brother in the succession wars.

The rest of the sons of Shah Jahan were dispatched throughout the empire to serve as viceroys and commanders. Even though they were far away from the throne, they gathered much-needed experience and support for the later clash with their brother. Shah Shuja, the second eldest, was appointed as the governor of Bengal and Orissa in 1638. Bengal was one of the richest and most powerful regions of the empire, and Shah Shuja built his base there. Shah Jahan's fourth son, Murad Bakhsh, proved to be inadequate as he often misjudged the situations in the regions appointed to him for governance, which were Multan, Kashmir, Deccan, Kabul, Malwa, and Gujarat.

Shah Jahan's third son, Aurangzeb, was the most successful of the three brothers who governed the empire. He commanded the forces of Deccan successfully, conquering the whole plateau. Even though Aurangzeb's military successes were important, he received much less recognition than all of his brothers. However, he gained the loyalty of the Mughal's most powerful and battle-hardened army, which fought the constant rebellions of the Deccan sultanates.

When Shah Jahan fell ill in September 1657, Dara proclaimed himself as his father's regent. Even though the emperor recovered fairly quickly, the three younger brothers had already conspired against Dara and made a pact. Together, they decided to attack Dara, and in 1658, the first battle occurred. Shah Shuja attacked Dara first, not waiting to be united with the forces of his brothers. Dara easily defeated him, and while Shuja fled back to Bengal, the forces of Murad Bakhsh and Aurangzeb attacked the imperial army of their eldest brother. This time, Dara lost, and Murad proclaimed himself emperor. However, it was Aurangzeb who pressed forward and imprisoned Shah Jahan in Agra. The emperor proposed peace and promised that he would divide the empire between his four sons.

However, Aurangzeb was too powerful, and he captured and executed Murad in 1661. And since he had already crushed Shuja in 1659, who was later assassinated while fleeing his brother's forces, he only had Dara left to deal with.

Defeated, Dara could only run, and he sought refuge in Punjab, Sindh, Gujarat, and Rajasthan, where he was finally defeated by Aurangzeb. Dara was captured and executed in 1662. After defeating all of his brothers, Aurangzeb kept his father Shah Jahan imprisoned in the fort of Agra. The old emperor had no real support of the army or the nobles of his court. Instead, he was attended by his favorite daughter Jahanara, who remained unmarried. Shah Jahan died in 1666 at the age of 74 from natural causes. Aurangzeb was already in full control of the Mughal Empire by this point, and there was no one left to challenge his right to the throne.

Aurangzeb (r. 1658–1707)

Aurangzeb

https://upload.wikimedia.org/wikipedia/commons/b/b3/Aurangzeb-portrait.jpg

Muhi-ud-Din Muhammad is more commonly known by his nickname Aurangzeb, "Ornament of the Throne," even though his regnal title was Alamgir, "Conqueror of the World." He ruled for 49 years, during which he expanded his empire and ruled almost the whole Indian subcontinent. He is considered to be the last effective ruler of the Mughal empire and the one who established Sharia law throughout India. Though he is praised for his military genius, he is also described as the most controversial ruler in Indian history.

Aurangzeb was 26 years old when he resigned from the governorship of the Deccan Plateau to pursue a life of religious devotion. However, after only six months, his father ordered him to resume his duties. Aurangzeb was extremely religious, and once he took the throne, he began cleansing the court of the unorthodox protocols of his predecessors. His goal was to make Islam the dominant religion in his empire, and he was relentless in his endeavors. Today, many scholars accuse him of the attempt to destroy the Bamiyan Buddhas when he tried to use cannons to bring down the statues. He managed to break the legs of the Buddhas before his attention was brought elsewhere. He severely punished the temples and schools of the Hindu Brahmins, a caste of Hindu priests, ordering their demolition throughout the provinces. Aurangzeb also punished the Muslims who didn't respect the Islamic laws on proper dressing, and he executed many Sufi mystics who opposed his endeavors to bring Islam to the forefront of the empire. Sikh Guru Tegh Bahadur was publicly killed in 1675 for resisting the forced mass conversion of Hindus to Islam.

Even though Aurangzeb introduced Sharia Law in the Mughal Empire, and despite his efforts to convert the non-Muslims, he employed more Hindu bureaucrats than any of his predecessors. Scholars believe that it was his successful campaign in Deccan back in 1656 and 1657 that caused the constant influx of Marathas (from present-day Maharashtra) to the Mughal Empire. One of the Rajput nobles was even known for the destruction of mosques in order to build Hindu temples, and in spite of knowing about this, Aurangzeb continued to work with him for the next two decades. Only the death of this Rajput ended their good relationship.

Since Aurangzeb's father led a very lavish life, causing Aurangzeb to inherit an almost empty royal treasury, Aurangzeb imposed a jizya in 1679. This was a military tax on non-Muslim citizens who did not fight for the Mughal Empire. However, women, children, the elderly, the handicapped, the ill, the mentally ill, monks, hermits, and slaves were all exempt from this new tax. Also, the non-Muslims who were only temporary residents (mainly the merchants) of the empire did not need to pay the tax. However, Hindu merchants had to pay their taxes at a higher rate than Muslims. In addition, all Hindus were removed from their offices in the revenue administration. There are contemporary historians who claim that the jizya was just a tax on paper that was forced on the people of the Mughal Empire.

Aurangzeb mainly ruled from the city of Shahjahanabad (Old Delhi) until 1679, when he left. He did not see this city ever again, nor did he ever come back to the territories of Hindustan. Until the end of his rule, Aurangzeb would move among military encampments or reside in the provisional capitals of certain regions to deal with emerging crises personally. Sometimes, he would even command the battles himself.

The Mughal emperor tried to meddle in the succession disputes of Rajasthan when he took the only surviving son of the dead Maharaja Jaswant Singh Rathore of Marwar. He converted the infant to Islam and named him Muhammadi Raj. He also selected a new leader for Marwar, an unpopular nephew of Jaswant Singh. The population objected to Aurangzeb's interference, and the clan of Rathore rebelled. Marwar was annexed because of this rebellion, which Aurangzeb personally oversaw. Neighboring Mewar had to quickly react unless they wanted the same destiny as Marwar, and the Sisodia clan of Mewar decided to join the rebellion.

Aurangzeb appointed his fourth son, Muhammad Akbar, as the commander of the Mughal armies that fought the rebels. However, in 1681, Akbar switched sides and joined the Marwars, proclaiming himself the new emperor. Akbar almost imprisoned his father, but his own Rathore allies were persuaded to betray him. Aurangzeb defeated his son, but instead of begging for forgiveness, Akbar sought refuge in the south at the court of the Maratha leader, Maharaja Sambhaji. Furious, Aurangzeb imprisoned his favorite daughter Zeb-un-Nissa, accusing her of conspiring with Akbar. After spending twenty years in prison, Zeb-un-Nissa died, but the year of her death is debated to be either 1701 or 1702. Once the Sisodia rana of Mewar died, his successor gave up on fighting Aurangzeb and ceded his territories. However, Marwar continued to fight the Mughal Empire, using guerilla warfare strategies, and the fighting continued until Aurangzeb's death in 1707.

Akbar continued to defy his father, even after they reconciled when Aurangzeb offered him forgiveness for the rebellion. Akbar launched failed raids into Hindustan and taunted his father, often reminding Aurangzeb of the fact that his own son had overthrown him. He also urged him to renounce the throne and go make the Hajj, an Islamic pilgrimage to Mecca. Akbar had to run away from his father's anger once more, and he fled to the court of the Safavid dynasty, just like his ancestors Babur and Humayun had done. However, unlike his ancestors, Akbar did not return to Hindustan as a conqueror. Instead, he died in exile in 1706, and he didn't live long enough to succeed his father.

Aurangzeb sent his second son, Muhammad Mu'azzam, to capture Hyderabad in the wealthy Golconda Sultanate, which he did in 1685. However, the sultan retreated to the impregnable Golconda Fort, and Mu'azzam wasn't able to defeat him. Convinced that his son had betrayed him, Aurangzeb took direct command of the forces, and it took him eight months to bring down the fortress. Mu'azzam, his wife, and his children were imprisoned for betrayal in 1687, and they were not released until 1695. When Golconda fell, the sultanate was annexed, and Aurangzeb took its rich treasury. The Muslims of the Golconda court were received into the Mughal military service, and they were given a mansab of 1,000 or higher, depending on their previous level of prestige.

During his seventies and eighties, Aurangzeb struggled to control his empire. The Mughals had expanded their territories to the point where the costs of the empire exceeded the benefits for its subjects. The emperor simply had no adequate administration, technology, or manpower to rule such a vast empire. Instead of continuing to expand the Mughal Empire, Aurangzeb was forced to satisfy his army by raiding the surrounding kingdoms. They would occasionally make those kingdoms pay a yearly tribute, but Aurangzeb was aware he could not afford to annex them and have their territories join with the already swollen Mughal Empire.

Aurangzeb knew he could not rule forever, but he was displeased with all of his sons and didn't consider any of them worthy of his throne. He continued to keep them bound to him through monetary allowances, often sending them to govern the lands that would bring the least revenue. By the time Aurangzeb had aged, and the time for deciding the succession was evident, none of his sons was strong enough to take the empire under his own rule. Because Aurangzeb had ruled for so long–he was 88 when he died–his sons were already old, with Mu'azzam being 63 and Azam, Aurangzeb's third youngest son, 54. So, the two princes were forced to wait until their father's death to be able to make their moves and fight for the throne.

Aurangzeb saw no other way to preserve his empire but to divide it between his sons. In his will, he dedicated the provinces of Agra, Ajmer, Aurangabad, Berar, Bidar, Gujarat, Khandesh, and Malwa to one son, while the other would get Delhi along with the provinces of Allahabad, Oudh (Awadh), Bengal, Bihar, Kabul, Kashmir, Multan, Orissa, Punjab, and Thatta. His only other surviving son, who was also the youngest, was the son of a low-born concubine. He already had Golconda and Bijapur under his command, and Aurangzeb asked Azam and Mu'azzam to respect their youngest brother, Muhammad Kam Bakhsh. However, the events that followed couldn't be controlled by Aurangzeb's sons or by any of the later emperors of the Mughal Empire. Many consider the year 1707, the year when Aurangzeb died, to be the last year of the Mughal Empire because, after this date, a series of weak emperors ruled. However, the dynasty continued, and the contemporary warlords and regional rulers recognized its importance, albeit nominally.

Chapter 6 – The Decline and Fragmentation of the Empire (1707–1857)

Stating in his will that the empire needed to be divided, Aurangzeb tried to spare his sons from the succession wars that he had to win when it was his time to rule. However, all three princes, Mu'azzam, Azam, and Kam Bakhsh, declared themselves the emperor of the whole Mughal Empire. Even though the brothers wanted to kill each other in the power struggle, none of them had control over a large military force. This was due to Aurangzeb lowering the salary of the mansabdars, causing commanders to protect their own interests. This doesn't mean they didn't recognize the legitimacy of the princes, and they avoided direct disobedience, but whenever it was possible, they avoided fighting other powerful commanders.

It was Mu'azzam that reached Shahjahanabad and Agra first, and by taking the royal treasuries there, he proclaimed himself Emperor Bahadur Shah I (r. 1707-1712). Soon, he clashed with Azam, who marched with his army from the Deccan Plateau to Shahjahanabad, but Azam was killed during the battle. The third son, Kam Bakhsh, fortified himself in Golconda, but in 1709, Bahadur Shah launched an attack and killed him, thus securing his throne.

After every succession struggle, the new ruler would need money, and Bahadur Shah was no exception. To get more wealth, he extracted more revenues than his predecessors. The territories that were controlled by his brothers were divided among his most loyal mansabdars as a reward. The Rajputs of Rajasthan and the Sikhs in Punjab took the opportunity of the power struggle to raise their own rebellions, and Bahadur Shah spent most of his ruling years in campaigns to quell them. However, the emperor lacked the bond his predecessors had with their mansabdars and subjects, and his four-year rule was just the beginning of the empire's downfall.

Bahadur Shah died of illness, probably due to the enlargement of his spleen, on February 27th, 1712, and a new succession war started. All of his four sons proclaimed themselves as the new emperor, just like Bahadur Shah and his brothers had done. In their desperation to gain the loyalty of the mansabdars, they spent enormous amounts of money on bribing the right people and spending it on their personal armies. In the beginning, the three brothers conspired to divide the empire between themselves once they killed the fourth, Azim-ush-Shan, who was more powerful than the others as he had accumulated much wealth as the governor of Bengal. However, once they killed Azim-ush-Shan, the three brothers turned against each other. Finally, after the bloodthirsty conflicts and fratricide had played out, the eldest, Muhammad Mu'izz-ud-Din, better known as his regnal title of Jahandar Shah, emerged victorious in 1713. However, within months, the son of the late Azim-ush-Shan, Muhammad Farrukhsiyar, marched his forces down the Ganges from Bengal and attacked his uncle. Near Agra, he defeated the imperial army and seized the throne for himself. During his rule, which lasted from 1713 to 1719, he struggled to hold the vast empire together.

The Salatin (1713–1859)

In 1713, Jahandar Shah created the Salatin, the slums of the Red Fort. The term was also used for all the Mughal princes who lived, along with their families, in the Red Fort, located in the city of Delhi. Emperor Jahandar Shah made them all prisoners of the Red Fort by confining them to slum-like quarters, and he passed a law that wouldn't allow the princes and the members of their families to leave the fort. Although they lived the shameful lives of prisoners, the people of the Mughal Empire still believed they held a privileged status.

Since each emperor had a large harem, the number of imprisoned relatives grew over time. The recorded number of Salatin in 1836 was 795, but by 1848, the number had increased to 2,104. All of them lived in the Red Fort and were guarded by eunuchs, who would lock them in their quarters during the night. Attempts to escape were made, but they were treated as criminals regardless. Some princes managed to escape, and they had to seek refuge in the neighboring kingdoms, where they were often treated as royal guests. However, those who remained in Salatin lived in perpetual poverty. Emperors did allow them small allowances, though, which would keep them dependent on their goodwill. However, that was not nearly enough money to keep the whole family alive. Instead, Salatins would often turn to moneylenders for help.

Oftentimes, the emperors would exhaust their riches, and they couldn't even pay the small allowance of one to five rupees per day to his imprisoned relatives. The amount of the allowance depended on how close a relative was to the ruling emperor. Salatins would protest with loud crying and wailing inside their home, which would drive the ruling emperor mad enough to borrow from moneylenders just to be able to pay his relatives. A British Army engineer, named Major Alexander Cunningham, visited the Red Fort, and he described how the Salatins lived. He recorded that a high wall was erected around the slums to keep the world of the Salatins very private. They lived in mat huts with only a few objects in their private possessions. They were all starved and half-naked. Among them were older people, some even in their eighties, and infants. Sometimes, they were given a few blankets to keep them warm during the cold months, and these were seen as an act of charity by the emperor.

At one point, the East India Company tried to resolve the issue of the Salatin but ultimately failed. They proposed to open a school within the walls of the Red Fort, in which they would educate the Mughal princes and give them the opportunity to find a job working for the Company. However, they couldn't guarantee a job for everyone, as there were so many of them. Those who wouldn't receive employment would just create additional problems for the Company, and so, the plan was abandoned. The Salatins were to stay imprisoned and all but forgotten.

When the last emperor of the Mughal Empire died in 1862, the Salatins were finally free to leave the Red Fort. Entire families wandered from one place to another, not being able to settle in the vast world that was completely unknown to them. It took time for them to finally disappear in the crowd, forgetting who they were. Occasionally, a family would claim they were the descendants of the Salatins, but no one was interested in them anymore. The world had changed, and the Mughal royal family meant nothing to the people.

During its decline, the emperor kept the nominal authority of the Mughal Empire; however, the effective military and political power were in the hands of prominent courtiers, commanders, and governors. Farrukhsiyar took the throne with the help of the governors of Allahabad and Bihar. They were actually brothers, Sayyid Abdullah Khan and Sayyid Husain Ali Khan Barha, and they were both excellent military tacticians. However, Farrukhsiyar had no riches to reward the brothers who supported his enthronement, and as he had no private army, he couldn't confront the Sayyid brothers. They posed a serious problem, as they threatened to enthrone another royal family member whenever Farrukhsiyar proved to be too demanding of their revenues. Farrukhsiyar schemed to lower the influence of the Sayyid brothers by favoring other mansabdars, most often Nizam-ul-Mulk, the leader of the Turani family that governed the territories in the Deccan Plateau.

Although Farrukhsiyar sought the support of the Rajputs and other Hindu commanders, some of them rebelled against him. Raja Ajit Singh Rathore expelled the Mughal officials from Marwar and Ajmer. He was aided by the Rajputs of Mewar and Amber, who also rebelled. Again, the emperor needed the help of the Sayyid brothers to quell the rebellions in the Deccan, and after succeeding, he married the daughter of Ajit Singh in 1715. However, he followed the example of his orthodox Muslim predecessor Aurangzeb, and he converted his new wife to Islam. Once she was widowed, she went through the purification ceremony and returned to Hinduism, becoming an avid opposer of the Mughal culture.

The Sayyid brothers continued to support Farrukhsiyar, but in reality, they were the true rulers. The emperor was just a figurehead, although he continuously tried to regain political power. As he had no power to manage the events that followed, he decided to spend most of his time hunting, writing poetry, and scheming to free himself from the too-powerful Sayyids, as well as from the influence of their powerful enemies. It is reported that the emperor tried to poison some of the most powerful mansabdars and that he would also appoint two men to the same office in the hopes that they would kill each other.

Finally, the Sayyid brothers had had enough of the emperor's efforts to dispose of them, and in 1719, they decided to overthrow him and place a more compliant emperor on the throne. They already had the reputation of being kingmakers due to their previous efforts to help Farrukhsiyar. On February 28th, they dragged the emperor out of his harem and blinded him. At first, they believed it was enough to just imprison Farrukhsiyar, but they changed their minds, and the emperor was assassinated on April 19th. In his place, the Sayyid brothers appointed Rafi ud-Darajat, the tenth Mughal emperor.

The Sayyid brothers destroyed the concept of an individual rule in the Mughal Empire, and their actions would be imitated by other powerful families of the Mughal court. In total, the Mughal court would see seven depositions in the next forty years. The Sayyids grasped too much power and created enemies who would unite against them. Even though both were assassinated in the times that followed, they created the pattern of kingmaking that would continue to happen under the supervision of various powerful commanders of the Mughal Empire. Some scholars even named them regents of the empire, though such a title was never officially given to them. All of the Mughal emperors who ruled after Farrukhsiyar were no more than puppets of their courtiers, and they were all chosen from the slums of the Salatin.

In the decades that followed the assassination of Farrukhsiyar, the Salatin emperors were constantly afraid for their lives. Kingmakers were ruthless in using these poor Mughal princes, enthroning them and disposing them at their will. Some of them were assassinated, while others were returned to the slums from which they came, grateful that their lives were spared. The majority of them ruled for only a few months, but there was one that ruled for almost thirty years, Muhammad Shah, though he was also one of the weakest Mughal emperors. None of the Salatin princes had any administrative knowledge or military experience to rule the empire, which made them perfect rulers for the powerful families of the empire who would ultimately control them.

Muhammad Shah (r. 1719-1748)

Muhammad Shah

https://en.wikipedia.org/wiki/Muhammad_Shah#/media/File:Mu%E1%B8%A5ammad_Sh%C3%A1h_on_horseback.jpg

Born Nasir-ud-Din Muhammad Shah, he was imprisoned together with his mother by his uncle, Jahandar Shah. He was only twelve when the succession war between his uncles and father took place, and even though he was confined in the slums of Salatin, his mother took care of his education and gave him the best she could. Perhaps this was the reason why the Sayyid brothers chose him as the emperor in 1719. After they disposed of Farrukhsiyar, several Salatin princes were chosen, but they only reigned for a few months before Muhammad Shah ascended the throne.

Muhammad Shah was enthroned in the Red Fort on September 29th, 1719, and like his predecessors, the Sayyid brothers kept him under strict supervision. Although he was free to finally leave Salatin and live the rich life of the emperor, Muhammad Shah wasn't free to make a single decision on his own. The first challenge to his throne happened the very next year, in 1720, when the political enemy of the Sayyid brothers, Nizam-ul-Mulk, later known as Asaf Jah I once he established the Hyderabad state and his own dynasty, chose Muhammad Ibrahim as the new Mughal emperor. However, both Asaf Jah and Ibrahim were quickly defeated by the ever-growing supporters of Muhammad Shah.

Although he was very young, Muhammad Shah was aware of the politics of the Sayyid brothers, and he strived to get rid of their influence. After the defeat of Muhammad Ibrahim, the Mughal emperor made a deal with Asaf Jah I, and Sayyid Husain Ali Khan was assassinated in October of 1720 as a consequence of that deal. Muhammad Shah now took full control over the Mughal army, and he sent Asaf Jah to take command of the Mughal provinces in the Deccan. Another noble, Muhammad Amin Khan Turani, was given a mansab of 8,000, and he was sent to confront Grand Vizier Sayyid Abdullah Khan. In the Battle of Hasanpur on November 15th, 1720, the second Sayyid brother was defeated and captured. The Mughal emperor would decide to execute him two years later.

Muhammad Shah was now finally free of the Sayyid brothers' influence; however, he lacked the knowledge of how to run his empire. Asaf Jah was appointed as the grand vizier, but when Muhammad Shah displayed an ultimate disinterest and inability to deal with the administration of the empire, Asaf Jah left the court in disgust. Instead of taking the opportunity to rule the Mughal Empire either from the shadows or by directly disposing of Muhammad Shah, Asaf Jah decided to take the territories of Deccan and founded his state of Hyderabad in 1724.

Even though Muhammad Shah had gained control of his empire by getting rid of the control imposed by the Sayyid brothers, he was still considered to be a weak ruler. During his reign, much of the destabilization of the Mughal Empire happened. For the most part, the emperor himself contributed to the problem due to his lack of knowledge and wisdom to run the state. The fragmentation of the empire, which began with the creation of Hyderabad State, would not stop. Although the decline of the empire could already be felt, it continued to be strong in at least one aspect: culture. Muhammad Shah was a great patron of the arts, and he was even famous for his writing, which he did under the pen name Sada Rangila, "Ever Joyous."

It was during his rule that Urdu replaced the Persian script, as Muhammad Shah proclaimed it to be the language of his court. He was a great patron of music, especially Sufi Islamic Qawwali, which was Sufi devotional music that gained popularity and spread throughout the empire and the rest of Southeast Asia. Muhammad Shah also opened schools, as he valued education, but he also translated the Quran in simple Persian and Urdu, thus making it available to the masses. The Quran was then taught in the elementary schools that Muhammad Shah opened, known as *maktabs.* Muhammad Shah spent riches employing famous artists, from painters to musicians. The arts were taught at the court, and it paved the road for the development of Indian classical music. In fact, the Mughal emperor spent more money investing in art than in the administration of the state, which only helped to ensure the later fragmentation of the government.

The Later Mughal-Maratha Wars, which lasted between 1728 and 1763, consisted of raids from Malwa that continuously devastated the north of the ill-administered Mughal Empire. These conflicts taught Muhammad Shah the importance of the empire's administration. He managed to get rid of the bad advisors who had multiplied around him after Asaf Jah left, and he was forced to adopt the skills of statesmanship. However, the fragmentation of his vast empire had already started, and he could do next to nothing to stop it. In the Punjab region, the Sikhs caused devastation with constant guerilla attacks on the Mughal officials who administered these territories. In Ajmer, a city in Rajasthan, the Marathas carved a large territory for themselves and claimed independence from the Mughal Empire. Also, the Deccan was under constant attacks, which led to the destruction of Mughal forts and only sped up the process of the decline of the empire. The Marathas even reached Delhi and raided it in 1737. When signing a peace treaty in Delhi in early 1738, Muhammad Shah ceded Malwa to the Marathas as one of its conditions.

By 1739, the Mughal Empire was weak enough to have become an attractive target for foreign opportunists. Nader Shah of Persia, drawn by the wealth and weakness of the Mughal Empire, launched an attack and captured Kabul, Ghazni, Lahore, and Sindh. At the Battle of Karnal in the same year, the forces of Muhammad Shah were defeated by the Persians in just three hours. The defeat was a hard blow to the Mughal Empire, as it opened the way to Delhi, which Nader Shah's army looted, depriving it of all its riches. The Battle of Karnal was just the start of the foreign invasions, which would continue to weaken the Mughal Empire and lead to its ultimate demise.

The first victory for the Mughal Empire happened in 1748 when they fought the invading Afghans under the leadership of Ahmad Shah Durrani. The Mughal forces were led by the heir apparent of Muhammad Shah, Ahmad Shah Bahadur, and he commanded 75,000 men. The Afghans, who numbered only 12,000, were easily defeated at the Battle of Manupur, and the Mughal Empire celebrated the long-needed victory for days.

The victory at the Battle of Manupur was paid with a heavy price, though. Many died, and the empire's army, although victorious, was devastated. Initially, the numbers of the dead were kept a secret, but once Muhammad Shah learned the truth, he closed himself in his quarters for three days. The emperor was so shocked he could not speak. He spent his days crying out loud, mourning his army. On April 16th, 1748, Muhammad Shah was found dead in his rooms, and it is recorded that he died of grief.

Chapter 7 – The Final Generations of the Mughals (1748–1857)

Ahmad Shah Bahadur was the son of the previous Mughal emperor, Muhammad Shah, and he to witnessed the decentralization of his father's empire, the conflicts with Maratha, and the invasion from the Persian ruler Nader Shah. Even though Ahmad Shah was the heir apparent, he was constantly belittled by his father, who never even gave him any education, military training, or an allowance worthy of a prince. By the time of his succession, Ahmad Shah Bahadur didn't know how to read or write and was a frequent visitor of the harem. During his rule, the empire was managed by his mother, Qudsia Begum, who entrusted state affairs to the head eunuch of the court.

Once Ahmad Shah was crowned on April 18th, 1748, in the Red Court, he was free from his father's bullying, and he could indulge in his passion for women without anyone stopping him. His love for the harem proved to be no more than a nuisance for his mother, who was given a mansab of 50,000. Under her influence, Ahmad Shah appointed Safdar Jang as the grand vizier, as he was the only able administrator, which he proved by governing Oudh and Kashmir.

Qudsia Begum also influenced the promotion of Javed Khan to the official title of Nawab Bahadur, or chief eunuch. Javed Khan had started as a harem eunuch and eventually progressed to the position of head eunuch of the royal household. It is speculated that because of his youthfulness, robust personality, and handsomeness, Qudsia Begum took him as a lover and had him promoted to become the regent of the Mughal Empire. Just as the Sayyid brothers took control of the many Mughal emperors, so, too, did Ahmad Shah's mother and Javed Khan.

Under the rule of Ahmad Shah Bahadur, the fragmentation of the Mughal Empire continued. The constant internal struggles for power between his regent Javed Khan and his opposition, led by Grand Vizier Safdar Jang, created the fertile ground for the further expansion of the Maratha Confederacy, which, in 1752, imposed a unilateral protectorate over the Mughal court in Delhi. Angered, Ahmad and his court had to retaliate, and in 1754, he launched an attack. The main battle was fought at Sikandarabad, which the Mughals lost, and their imperial household was humiliated. The Mughal emperor fled the battlefield, leaving his mother, wives, and 8,000 women to be captured by Feroze Jung III, better known as Imad-ul-Mulk, a Mughal military commander who had defected and joined the Marathas. Then, Imad-ul-Mulk proceeded to Delhi, where he killed Javed Khan and imprisoned and blinded Emperor Ahmad Shah Bahadur. He was proclaimed as the grand vizier of the Mughal Empire, and he decided to release Prince Aziz-ud-Din from the slums of the Salatin and overthrow Ahmad. The destiny of Qudsia Begum is unknown, but Ahmad Shah was allowed to live until his natural death in 1775. Thrown in the Salatin, he was too poor and wretched to live past the age of 49.

Aziz-ud-Din is better known by his regnal name of Alamgir II. He was the second son of Jahandar Shah, and he ruled the remnants of the Mughal Empire from 1754 until 1759. At the time of his succession, Alamgir was already an old man, as he was almost 55, and he had no administrative or military experience. He was yet another perfect puppet emperor of the too-powerful Mughal courtiers and their families. Imad-ul-Mulk conspired with the Maratha Confederacy, which grew stronger with each passing year. During the reign of Alamgir II and Grand Vizier Imad-ul-Mulk, the Marathas were at the peak of their expansion, which came at the cost of an already weak Mughal Empire.

In the effort to escape the influence of Imad-ul-Mulk, Alamgir II made an alliance with the Durrani Empire (today's territories of Afghanistan and Pakistan) in 1755 and their leader, Ahmad Shah Durrani, who was in Lahore at the time. The Durrani shah and his forces marched to Delhi to get rid of Imad-ul-Mulk and his Maratha allies. Upon arriving, the royal family of Alamgir II met the Durrani leaders, and to strengthen the pact against the Mughal grand vizier, Ahmad's son, Timur Shah Durrani, was engaged to Alamgir's daughter, Zuhra Begum. Ahmad retreated to Kabul, leaving his forces under his son's charge.

However, the Marathas rejected the alliance between the Mughal emperor and the Durrani Empire, and in 1757, they began the siege of Delhi. They made a camp thirty kilometers (almost 19 miles) away from the Red Fort and occupied the surrounding villages, which provided for the Maratha army. The Mughals had only 2,500 soldiers garrisoned inside Delhi, but by positioning heavy artillery on the walls, they were able to resist the attacks for the next five months. However, the help of the Durrani never came, as Ahmad Shah Durrani was too busy fighting resistance in his own empire. After the Marathas managed to cut off the food supply to the city of Delhi, its commander, Naib-ul-Daula, eventually had to surrender and proclaim defeat.

When the Marathas entered the city, they expected to capture the emperor and his royal family, but somehow, Alamgir managed to escape, and he was received as a royal refuge in the Hindu Kingdom of Bharatpur. With the help of Suraj Mal, the ruler of Bharatpur, Alamgir II returned to Delhi with his royal family. Imad-ul-Mulk conspired to assassinate Alamgir II and his whole family, but word of his plans reached the prince and heir, Ali Gohar, who managed to escape. However, he did not save his father; whether this was by choice is not known. Alamgir II was killed in late November 1759, and Imad-ul-Mulk was free to choose the new emperor who would become his puppet. For that role, he chose Shah Jahan III, who ruled for only one year before he was deposed by the Marathas.

The next and sixteenth emperor of the Mughals was Ali Gohar, better known as Shah Alam II, who ruled from 1760 until 1788. As mentioned above, he was the son of Alamgir II and managed to escape Delhi when the plot to assassinate his father became evident to him. He was chosen as the emperor of the Mughal Empire by Ahmad Shah Durrani, who helped him defeat Imad-ul-Mulk and his Maratha allies. However, the Mughal Empire was now reduced to Delhi and the small surrounding areas around the city. The Persians had a saying, "Sultanat-e Shah Alam, Az Dilli ta Palam," which means "The empire of Shah Alam is from Delhi to Palam." Palam remains a suburb of Delhi to this day.

However, Shah Alam wouldn't let his empire to be reduced to only one city. Immediately after succeeding the throne, he tried to restore his authority over Bihar and Bengal. He ordered the submission of the governor of Bengal, who was no more than the puppet figure for the British East India Company. The Company wouldn't surrender its interests to a weak Mughal emperor, and since they owned a private British army, they resisted Alam's advances. Shah Alam invaded Bihar on three occasions, but his army of 30,000 soldiers was no match for the rich British commanders who were determined to stay.

The Mughals were used to Europeans by now as they had fought with or against the Portuguese, who came to these parts of the world as traders. The French followed the Portuguese as the demand for Indian goods grew throughout Europe. The British were the last to come; however, their tactics were significantly different from their European predecessors. The British East India Company never hid the fact that they wanted to get involved in the politics of the Indian subcontinent. Not that the French and Portuguese did not get involved, but they always came with trade as the main reason for their presence in these regions.

During much of the 16th and 17th centuries, trade was indeed the main focus of the East India Company. However, with the decline of the Mughal Empire, their focus shifted to owning its territory. Bengal came under British rule during the Carnatic Wars, which lasted from 1746 to 1763. When the British commanders defeated the Nawabs of Bengal in the Battle of Buxar in 1764, the Company was in full control of the Bengal territory and had all the rights to collect its revenue. The East India Company thus became a major political power in the Indian subcontinent. It had either direct control over the territories it ruled or had it through puppet rulers and governors who were under constant military pressure from the British.

The Company's army wasn't composed of actual British soldiers for the most part. In fact, they hired Indian infantrymen, who were then trained in the European style of warfare. They were called sepoys. Sepoys were always commanded by Europeans, who brought technologically advanced artillery with them, allowing them to easily triumph over the much larger Mughal army.

Once Shah Alam II submitted himself to the East India Company in 1763, the British had even more legitimacy to the rule of the Indian subcontinent. However, Shah Alam wasn't happy with the situation; although he was a weak ruler, he constantly strived for the greatness of his much earlier predecessors. By 1764, he had escaped the British and joined his forces with Shuja-ud-Daulah, the Nawab of Oudh, who previously helped him attack Bengal and Bihar. They tried to invade these territories once again, and the losses they suffered at the Battle of Buxar in 1764 and the Battle of Kora in 1765 were devastating. Shah Alam was again forced to accept the Company as his superior, but he did manage to negotiate a settlement. The Company returned the province of Allahabad to the Mughal emperor, and they promised him an annual tribute of 2,600,000 rupees (today, this sum would be around forty million

British pounds). In exchange, Shah Alam allowed whomever the East India Company chose to govern Bengal and Bihar. He also appointed the Company as his diwan in these territories. Diwan was a title used for various offices of the states, and to the Company, it brought legal power to collect revenues in Bengal and Bihar, but it would take the Court of Directors of the East India Company another six or seven years to officially accept the title.

Shah Alam wasn't really satisfied with the deal he made with the East India Company in the Treaty of Allahabad, and he sent a mission to England, pleading King George III to install him back on the throne of Hindustan. He promised that the British king's name would be celebrated throughout the Indian subcontinent and that he would be in personal debt to the British ruler if he officially enthroned him in his former capital of Shahjahanabad (Old Delhi). However, the complex negotiations between the East India Company and the British Parliament thwarted the Mughal mission, and the ambassador who was tasked with it was never presented to the king. The Mughal ambassador, I'tisam-ud-Din, returned to Hindustan in 1769, and besides his report to the emperor, he also wrote the first Indian book about Britain, the travel narrative *Shigurf-nama-i-Wilayat*, "Wonder Book of England."

In 1770, the East India Company paid only 18 percent of their promised annual tribute to Shah Alam II, and in 1772, they paid 23 percent. Yet the Mughal emperor had no other choice but to remain under British protection. The reason might be due to his own weakness and inability to claim what was his by right, or it might have been due to the fact that even such a low amount of money was still a much higher income for the emperor than what he received decades before. Also, aside from some minor issues with the reception protocol, the British officials treated the Mughal emperor with much more respect than his previous regents, the Sayyid brothers, Imad-ul-Mulk, and Ahmad Shah Durrani.

However, Shah Alam II continued to dream of restoring his empire. He begged the East India Company to help him retrieve

Shahjahanabad, where much of his court and household remained, but they refused. The Mughal emperor then searched for help elsewhere. In 1771, he gave four million rupees to the Marathas to help him gain control of his previous capital. In addition, he promised the revenues of Allahabad and some other imperial cities. However, even though the military campaign was set out, nothing was achieved. Shah Alam struggled for the next three decades to return the lost glory of the Mughal Empire back, but the political scene of northern India was constantly shifting and changing due to foreign influence. The British East India Company had its own war with the French and could care less about the Mughal emperor. As such, the warlords and regional powers constantly changed, and the emperor lost what little control of the administration of his empire he held in his hands.

In 1788, one of the warlords, Ghulam Qadir, forced Shah Alam II to make him the grand vizier. He had the reputation of an insane person as he was constantly in search of Mughal riches, which he estimated to be around 250 million rupees. He ravaged the Mughal palaces located across the empire in search of these riches, and angered that he could not find anything, he blinded the emperor. Ghulam Qadir was brutal to the already elderly Shah Alam, as well as his family. Anyone who tried to help the bleeding emperor was beheaded. It is also recorded that Ghulam Qadir often pulled the emperor's beard to torture him. He made all of the Mughal princesses dance naked in front of him, after which they all jumped in the Yamuna River to drown.

With Ghulam Qadir as the grand vizier, the honor and prestige of the Mughal Empire was at its lowest. Finally, on October 2nd, 1788, Mahadaji Shinde, the Maratha ruler of Gwalior, killed Ghulam Qadir, taking Delhi under his protection. He restored Shah Alam II to the throne, which was now under the direct protection of the Maratha Confederacy. The Marathas ruled northern India for the next fifteen years, with a garrison permanently occupying Delhi. It was their conflict with the British East India Company in 1803 that overthrew their supremacy in the Mughal Empire.

As a result of the conflict, the East India Company conquered Shahjahanabad and its surrounding regions in 1803, but they still recognized Shah Alam II as the sovereign of the Mughal Empire. However, the emperor was forbidden to engage in the politics of his empire, and in turn, he was given a moderate sum of money as a pension. Shah Alam died in 1806, and his son Akbar II (r. 1806-1837) succeeded the Mughal throne. He, too, was confined in the court of Shahjahanabad and had no power to influence the political events of his empire. He was yet another puppet emperor controlled by the East India Company.

Still, the name of the Timurid emperors was respected by all Indians, and the Mughal court remained an attractive destination to many, whether they were Muslim, Hindu, or British. Although he had no political power, Akbar II managed to preserve the cultural life of Delhi, and the arts was the one thing that kept flourishing during the rule of the last three Mughal emperors. Like his predecessor, Akbar II was a poet, and he invested much in the culture of his crumbling empire. In recognition of his sovereignty, the East India Company issued coins with Persian script and his name. However, he was never more than a prisoner of the Company. In 1835, they even took away his title of emperor, and named him "King of Delhi." It was then that the Company stopped issuing the coins with his name and made all script of the coins in English alone.

However, the Company wasn't ready to proclaim themselves the nominal rulers of the northern Indian territories. Instead, they encouraged the Nawab of Oudh and the Nizam of Hyderabad to take the royal titles and be their puppet rulers. This would further diminish the influence Akbar II still had as the emperor of the Mughals.

When Akbar II died in 1837, the Company enthroned his eldest son, Bahadur Shah II, as their puppet ruler. He was already 62 at the time, and he was happy to stay out of the political life of the empire.

In 1850, the British decided that Bahadur Shah would be the last emperor of the Mughals. Their plan was to give the title of prince to Bahadur's heir and force the royal family to retire to a rural retreat that had been specially made for them. However, a massive uprising happened in India in 1857, and Bahadur Shah, even though he was 82, found himself in the middle of current political events.

In May 1857, unsatisfied by the British Christian rule, the Indian sepoys, rulers, and landholders, both Muslim and Hindu, revolted. The old peoples of northern India resented the intrusive lifestyle of the British newcomers, who imposed new social reforms, taxes, and harsh treatment of the natives. They wanted to restore the old Mughal Empire, and the main force of the rebelling army was concentrated around Bahadur Shah II, who the rebels proclaimed as their emperor. The rebels were successful in driving the British out of Shahjahanabad and much of northern India. However, after four months of bloody fighting, the British Army and the Indians who still obeyed them managed to recapture the main city and imprison the last Mughal emperor. After killing all of his sons, the British officers put the old emperor on trial for treason against the East India Company.

The life of emperor Bahadur Shah II was spared, but he and his whole family were exiled to Burma, where he died in 1862. The British rule of the Shahjahanabad destroyed many of the Mughal cultural monuments, as the military officers needed the area around the Red Fort cleared so the artillery on the walls would have a clear view. The Company also desecrated many of the Muslim and Hindu praying sites by celebrating Christian services in them. One of the famous mosques of the city, Jami' Mosque, was entirely destroyed.

Chapter 8 – Memory of the Mughal Empire

The Common People

The world of the Mughal Empire was a world of duality. Where the small number of elite nobles lived their lives preoccupied with wars and court intrigues, the common people of the Indian subcontinent worked to provide for both themselves and the elite. The emperor, his family, and the nobles were rich, and they enjoyed a life filled with art, music, and literature, but the common people of India were illiterate, exhausted, and often starving. While the court life of the Mughal nobles seemed unreachable, it was very much real. However, the greater reality was the barren life of the commoners.

The life of an average Indian in the Mughal Empire advanced little from the conditions in which their predecessors lived a thousand or more years earlier. The houses for the commoners were usually one-room hovels, with the floor made out of beaten earth covered in cow dung. Walls were made out of mud and the roof out of straw. The hovels were just high enough for a man to walk in bent at the waist. The hovels had no windows or doors, just one small opening that served as the entrance and exit. Usually, the commoner would share this hovel with his whole family and livestock if he had any.

Many European travelers were shocked by the duality of the Indian world. While emperors and nobles built grand palaces and temples out of various types of stones and bricks, the common people lived in small decrepit huts built of mud and wood. They had no need for more, for unlike emperors and nobles, the common people spent their days working in the fields, with their livestock, or crafting goods. The women cooked outside, and the children played outside. The inside of the hovels was more protection from the weather, night, and wild beasts, and nothing more. The Europeans often compared these huts to the cells of the prisons of Europe. However, in India, they were the reality of everyday life.

It should be noted that India did have a middle class during the Mughal Empire. Though their numbers were low, and they could hardly be noticed among the masses of poor commoners, the middle class did exist, and they had a better quality of life. While the commoners slept on the floor, which was often muddy, the middle class slept in makeshift hammocks. Due to the constant heat of India, they rarely used any blankets. Their houses, even though they were larger and better, had no tables or chairs; everyone sat on the ground. No one could afford tablecloths or even plates, and both commoners and the middle class used fig leaves to eat from. The same leaves were used as bed sheets or other linen. Even liquid could be held in the leaves, which were joint in such a masterful way that there was no leakage. Pots and other kitchen utensils were mostly made out of earthenware, and only a few of the middle class could afford a copper drinking cup.

What shocked the Christian Europeans the most was the way Indians, both Muslim and Hindu, dressed. The poorest of the commoners, both men and women, had only a piece of cloth tied to their waistline, which was big enough to cover their private parts. Women would sometimes cover their heads if they had extra material from their waistcloth. Since Europeans and the founder of the Mughal Empire, Babur, described Indian clothing the same way, it would appear that nothing changed in over two centuries. The Jesuits were especially shocked that Indians thought it was normal to pray to their gods half-naked. Only the soldiers had a bit more clothing, as well as a cloth tied around their heads. Laborers, commoners, and some soldiers had an extra piece of cloth that would serve them as a garment during the day and as bed linen during the night. This way, they were ready to sleep wherever they found themselves. It was usually the people of the middle class who could afford to wear a short shirt; sometimes, it would even be made of silk. However, no one except the nobles could afford shoes.

In the regions of India that are known for colder climates, the people wore more clothes. In Kashmir, it was common for both men and women to wear woolen tunics, and in the regions of Varanasi, the people were described wearing silk dhotis and scarfs. How people dressed was greatly determined by the region where they lived and its climate. What common people saved on clothing, they spent on ornaments and jewelry. European travelers through the Mughal Empire describe that families would rather die of hunger than have no ornaments to show off. Men also used their hairs as a type of ornament, especially Hindus, who wore it long and tied it to the side of their head. Muslims, especially Shia Muslims, shaved their heads. They also preferred beards, while the Hindus usually had only mustaches.

Just like their huts and their clothing, the food of the commoners was very poor. In the Mughal Empire, most Hindus were not vegetarians, but hardly anyone could afford meat. Usually, their meals would be grain-based, often with added greens, and mixed with rice. Indians had one big meal a day, usually at midday. The dish was rice-based, and the coastal people would often have a piece of dried fish as well. The meat from goats, chickens, or sheep was reserved for the nobles, and the commoners would eat it only during festivities. Europeans describe beef as being the cheapest meat in India, but no Hindu would eat it, as the cow was their sacred animal.

However, Muslims were allowed to eat beef, although they regarded beef as lesser. Emperors Akbar and Jahangir prohibited the slaughter of cows, and during their reigns, beef wasn't available to anyone. Furthermore, the peacock was a sacred bird, and shellfish was considered impure by both Muslims and Hindus. Pig meat was a taboo for the Muslims, but Hindus ate it if they could afford it. It was usually served to the Hindu nobles, though. However, hunting wasn't prohibited for the common people, and if they could catch a wild animal, they would eat it. Wheat was too expensive for the commoners, so they did not make bread out of it. Their main protein and other nutrients sources were from legumes, millets, and rice.

Although cows were sacred to Hindus, that doesn't mean they weren't useful. They still provided milk, and the people would use raw milk in their food or make butter and ghee out of it. However, milk wasn't the only product from cows that they would drink. In Mughal India, it was considered a sacred thing to drink a cow's urine. People would scoop the urine with their hands and take a sip, then wash their faces with the rest of it. By doing so, they would be able to proclaim themselves as cleansed and holy.

Although both Muslim and Hindu citizens of the Mughal Empire had their own taboos and generally didn't indulge in vices, both societies were very open toward sex. European travelers were shocked to learn that Indians didn't bother to hide when they consummated their marriages. The upper-class men basically had the right to take whichever woman they wanted, even if she was married to someone else. Muslim women were kept pure, but they, too, would secretly indulge in romantic relationships outside of their marriage. Muslim men, on the other hand, were allowed just about anything. They would often use children as old as seven or eight, and among nobles, homosexuality was normal. Hindus regarded homosexuality as wrong as eating beef, and it was unheard of in their society, although incest would happen, albeit very rarely, and even then, it would be punished.

Prostitution, on the other hand, was a very common thing in India, although each emperor had his own opinion on it. While Akbar set up a camp for the prostitutes and ordered all of their customers to be recorded, Emperor Shah Jahan allowed them everywhere and was even a frequent guest of the brothels. Hijras, the hermaphrodites for which India is known for even today, were very common during the Mughal period, and the Jesuits would beg the Mughal emperors to ban them, for which they were often laughed at.

Harems and the Position of Women

In Arabic, harem means a sacred, prohibited space. It was a common practice to include a harem in the courts of the Mughal Empire, and it was there that the women of the household lived. Their world was essentially vacuum-sealed and private, but harems were not exclusive to the imperial palaces. Households of notable nobles and state officials, both Muslim and Hindu, had their own harems. Traditionally, in India, women were not secluded or veiled until the Rajputs adopted the practice by imitating their Muslim superiors. Even then, purdah, the practice of veiling women to hide them from the sight of strangers, was not enforced on women; it was more of a status symbol for wealthy families. In some areas of the Mughal Empire, even Muslim women didn't veil themselves, for example, in the Deccan sultanates. In the territories of Kerala, women were not just free to do whatever they wanted, but they also held immense power, just like the men did.

Among the poor, there was no seclusion for the women. Since life was so basic, they couldn't allow for the dividing of men from women. Female Hindu and Muslim commoners had to work and earn their own living, and the hot climate of India prevented working men and women from wearing more clothes than necessary to cover their private parts. However, the ruling class was divided into two separate worlds, one of the men and the other of women. The women from rich and powerful families were often confined in their apartments and mansions. They were guarded jealously and were burned alive when the man of the house died, though this practice was mainly tied to Hindu culture.

For the ruling class, women were property, although a very valuable one. For a noblewoman, known as a begum, such life was desired above all, as they were treated well and often with respect. Even though they were property, women observed their seclusion as a privilege, not a punishment. In rare moments, they were allowed outside of the palaces and mansions, although the noble women of Muslim culture had to wear a burka, a loose garment that would cover their whole body, even the head. If they traveled to accompany their men, women were carried in covered litters, and no one was allowed to set eyes on them. Emperors never allowed a building to be built anywhere near the harem so that the sacred place could not be looked at. In fact, the jealousy of the Mughals went so far that husbands wouldn't allow their fathers-in-law or brothers-in-law to speak with their daughters and sisters unless they were present.

If a begum allowed herself to be seen in public, it meant either divorce or death. Divorce was no better as it almost certainly meant death, for her own family would denounce her. Even if she accidentally revealed herself, death was the only honorable way out for her. However, looking at royal women was not the only taboo in the world of the Mughal Empire. To speak a royal woman's name was also considered to be forbidden. To the outside world, these women were nameless, and women considered that to be the highest honor. Still, begums did exist, and in order to refer to them, people had to come up with beautiful epithets that would substitute their true names.

It is wrongly presumed that the imperial harem of the Mughal emperors was only reserved for his wives and concubines. In fact, the harem was a place where all the women of the household lived, which included queens, mothers, sisters, and closer or distant relatives. The harem had its guards, administrators, cooks, and servants, and the emperor would appoint his favorite begum as the head of the harem. Aside from the lavish life provided by the palace, each begum would receive her salary, and in the Mughal world, the amount of money they received varied based on their position and value to the emperor. It could be anywhere between 3 to 1,600 rupees a month. Some women received more money than a Mughal soldier would. With their money, begums were able to build tombs, temples, and other monuments in the glory of the empire. Some women were great patrons of art, while others cherished education.

Another wrong belief is that Mughal emperors had thousands of women in their harems who were there just for their satisfaction. Although the harems were vast and many women lived there, the emperors were simply people with the same needs just like any other men. They could not possibly waste their days in the harem, and they usually had only one favorite wife they would often go to. The harem was a symbol of power in the Mughal Empire, and that is why they were so large. Polygamy also wasn't just an excuse for pleasure. The emperor could have multiple wives for political reasons or as a favor to his best officers. Royal marriages were often enforced by peace treaties or alliances. Polygamy also occurred to ensure many children and, most importantly, to produce an heir to the Mughal throne. In that period of history, especially in Hindustan, children were often lost due to diseases that had no cures, or they would be killed in one of the many wars.

The emperors spent most of their days inside the harem, but it is wrong to believe that it was for pleasure. In fact, the emperor's offices were in the harem, and many women who lived there held their own offices, which were sometimes even equivalent to the office in the outside world. Women of the harem were educated, and they were the ones who did the administrative work of the empire. The harem is where emperors did their most confidential work, and they would often rely on the women to help. Women of the harem were often included in the business of the government, especially if the business was a family matter. The begums were allowed to attend meetings, although behind walls, curtains, or screens, so that they would be familiar with the matters of the state. These women often used their wits and cunning to manage the empire alongside the emperors. And often, they used their influence to steer politics the way they wanted. There was no better place to persuade the emperor than in the confined apartments of the harem.

The rich life of a begum provided the royal women with everything they wanted and more. However, they were greatly deprived of life, or at least that's how modern readers would see it. Mughal princesses didn't marry, as Emperor Akbar proclaimed that no man was worthy of a Mughal woman. Confined in their golden cage, the Mughal royal women had no family. They were basically taken away from their parents and locked away, never to see their brothers and sisters again. Only the privileged wives had children, and even those children were often taken away to be brought up in other parts of the empire. All the luxuries they enjoyed could not compensate for the loneliness they must have felt. To fill their days, many women occupied themselves with arts and crafts, such as embroidery, stitching, painting, and writing. Music and dancing were allowed as well in the harem, but some of the emperors would frown upon it, as the Muslim culture was against it.

The begums were the silent and invisible power that ran politics from behind the throne. Royal women wielded great power, and as such, they influenced events. It is no wonder they saw their place in the harem as prestigious and not as a punishment or form of bondage. Muslims denied women from playing a public role, but from the harem, a woman could have as much power as the emperor himself. However, being away from the public eye meant many of the great women of the Mughal Empire remain unknown to history. Although some were so exceptional that their names were recorded and remembered, most of them are lost to the past. The most remarkable of the Mughal queens is certainly Nur Jahan, the wife of Emperor Jahangir. She was even recognized as the real force behind the throne while her husband indulged in opium. She is the first and only queen of the Mughal Empire that has coins issued in her own name.

Culture

Illustration by the 17th-century Mughal artist Ustad Mansur
https://upload.wikimedia.org/wikipedia/commons/thumb/d/d3/Mansur-8.png/800px-Mansur-8.png

Culture flourished during the 16th and 17th centuries when the Mughals were at the height of their power in northern India. As patrons of many arts, it is no wonder the Mughal period is one of the most fruitful when it comes to culture. Not only did the Muslim culture enjoy the patronage of the Mughal emperors, but so did the Hindus. It is during this period that Hindu poetry, and literature in general, came to its heights.

Although Muslim and Hindu cultures coexisted in the Mughal Empire for a very long time, they influenced each other very little. Any influence that did happen was only superficial. This was due to the serious social segregation between the ruling Muslims and the subjected Hindus. While the Muslims observed Hindu culture as less important and not worthy of their attention, Hindus did not allow the Muslim way of life to influence their conservative society. Instead, they shaped their culture around Islam, being careful not to mix the two.

The Mughals generally came from a very abundant cultural background, and they enjoyed the intellectual and artistic achievements of their people. After all, they came from Central Asia, a territory that is known for mixing the cultures of three of the great civilizations of classic times, India, China, and Greece. Growing up with such traditions, the Mughal emperors themselves were multi-talented. Some of them are even known for their great cultural achievements. Babur, the founder of the Mughal Empire, was an accomplished author, composer, and calligrapher. Humayun was a lover of natural sciences and a great mathematician, astronomer, poet, and inventor. Akbar was a philosopher with a different set of skills, which included poetry, architecture, and music. Aurangzeb was the only Mughal emperor who didn't appreciate culture and had no skills of his own. But, as if to compensate for her father's inability in the field of arts, his daughter, Zeb-un-Nissa, was an avid patron of all kinds of arts and education.

The reign of Emperor Akbar was the most exciting time for culture, mainly in the field of science. Akbar and his subjects had a habit of looking toward the future of the empire, and for this, they were mocked by the traditionalists who found comfort in the past. But it was during his reign that science prospered, as people with ideas were valued above all. Natural sciences and medicine were very popular fields, and the emperor himself was very interested in the European discoveries in these disciplines. Although Akbar invested in bringing European technologies to the empire, mainly into the Mughal military, the people of India were generally not interested in anything European. Thus, the emperor couldn't instill the values of European sciences and crafts to his people. The best his people could do was mimic foreign products, which led to low-quality items. Indians never showed much interest in learning European technology and applying that knowledge to advance their own culture.

As patrons of the arts, the emperors expected artists to please them. This is why it was very hard for Mughal artists to express themselves or develop new techniques. All they could do was what their masters and employers wanted. They could not risk displeasing the nobles as they would risk not just their wellbeing but also their lives. An angry emperor could always order an artist to be executed. It was the same for the practitioners of medicine. If they were unable to cure a prominent officer or even emperor, they faced the prohibition of their practice or even execution.

Literature was highly valued in the Mughal Empire, and it was never really censored. Even when it portrayed a noble or a ruler in a bad light, the authors were never punished. Satire in literature was observed as a commentary on the events and persons, and it would often be taken as such. However, neither Muslim nor Hindu authors practiced mocking the rulers openly. Books and scripts were treated as treasures, and whenever a city was conquered, the libraries were treated with the utmost respect. Even though entire cities were burned as a display of power, the Mughal emperors would first loot them, and the books were a part of that loot, safely packed for transportation to the royal library. Even prominent women of the harem had their own libraries, and ladies, such as Jahanara and Zeb-un-Nissa, had some of the richest libraries of the Mughal Empire.

Poetry was so popular that the nobles often exchanged letters written in verse. When challenging another to a duel, one would write it down in verse, and the reply would also be in the form of poetry. Even though Emperor Akbar was illiterate or dyslexic, he kept a library that contained over 24,000 volumes. He employed people to read to him, and not just official letters and documents but books and poetry as well.

However, the most prominent artistic achievements of the Mughal Empire lay in its architecture, although the Mughals did not contribute much to the originality of the architecture but to its refinement instead. Their buildings were inspired by the Persian culture. They weren't even the first to introduce the Persian style into the architecture of India as the Delhi Sultanate did it before the Mughals. However, what is special about Mughal architecture is the degree of its refinement. Even today, Mughal buildings and monuments belong in another class by themselves.

Landscaping and gardening were other passions of the Mughal emperors, and even though the principle of public parks and gardens was known to India before the Mughals, they were the ones who extensively refined it. The gardens were a great love of the Mughals, and wherever they chose to stop, usually for weeks or months at a time, a garden had to be erected. The Mughals also introduced new plant and animal species into the Indian world, first from their native Central Asia and later on from Europe and the Americas. The gardens were places of relaxation and contemplation, a delightful piece of heaven on the ruthless and hot earth. The Mughal gardens were square or rectangular in their base and were divided into partitions, always using straight lines, never curves. They would create a grid, as in a network of passages, and in between them, they would landscape. The water was often directed through the garden, and it would freshen up the pleasant air, which was already rich with oxygen and exotic scents of various plants.

The nobles lived in vast, open buildings, and they cherished the open view, so no large trees were planted outside the palaces and mansions. While Hindu architecture reflected the conservative hidden lifestyle of its people, Mughal buildings were huge, cheerful, and reflected the adventurous lives of the Central Asians. They were richly decorated with paintings and stone carvings. The Mughals loved arches and latticed windows, which were always open, allowing the daylight and night breeze to play in the vast hallways and rooms. Unlike the Mughal structures, Hindus built small, dark, and airless rooms in which they felt safely confined.

Akbar was the first emperor who dared to combine the Persian and Indian styles of architecture. He built many buildings, of which the most famous were the Agra Fort and the elegant pavilion bridge across the Gomati River near the city of Jaunpur. Akbar usually chose red sandstone for his buildings, and marble was used only as a decoration, never as a building material. The ornaments of Akbar's buildings were usually low relief stone carvings and paintings on plastered surfaces. It was only with the reign of Shah Jahan that gem inlays became the hallmark of Mughal architecture. Apart from forts and palaces, the emperors built mosques and tombs, which were as rich as any other Mughal building. Gardens were part of every Mughal structure, be it a mansion, palace, mosque, or even a tomb. In fact, tombs of the Mughal royal family were often the centerpieces of a vast garden.

Certainly, the most famous tomb, and a staple of Mughal architecture, is the Taj Mahal, which was built as a resting place for Mumtaz Mahal, the favorite wife of emperor Shah Jahan. However, the Taj Mahal, although beautiful, brought nothing new to Mughal masonry. The inspiration for the most famous tomb was drawn from previous Mughal building achievements, specifically the tombs of Timur, the progenitor of the dynasty, and Humayun's tomb with its gardens.

The Taj Mahal in Agra, India
https://en.wikipedia.org/wiki/Mughal_Empire#/media/File:Taj_Mahal_(Edited).jpeg

The Taj Mahal is a complex of buildings in a beautiful garden. The tomb is just the central part of this complex, and it is built completely in white marble. Other buildings are mausoleums for Shah Jahan's other wives, a mosque, and a building that may have served as a guesthouse. The garden has its main gate, a monument constructed of marble, and vast pathways with a lake in the middle. The tomb of Mumtaz Mahal and Shah Jahan himself is a symmetrical building with a square base and an arch-shaped doorway. It is topped with a large white dome, and it has four minarets that serve as a frame for the tomb.

Both external and internal decorations of the Taj Mahal are the finest examples of Mughal artistry. The tomb is richly decorated with paintings, stone carvings, and calligraphy. The elements in these are mostly flora or abstract forms, as Islam prohibits anthropomorphic forms. The complex is inscribed with passages from the Quran, which serve both as decoration and as a lesson. The inside of the tomb goes well beyond the traditional decorative elements, as precious and semi-precious stones were used to create masterful works. The interior dome is decorated with the painted sun motif, and it has special openings for light to enter.

Many myths envelop the construction of the Taj Mahal. A story of the twin tombs of the Taj Mahal being built from black stone dates from 17th-century European travelers. Some say how everyone who was involved in the construction of the Taj Mahal had to sign a contract stating that they would not work on a similar design in the future. Others tell stories of how Shah Jahan punished and mutilated the workers and artisans who displeased him. There was even a theory that the Taj Mahal was designed by an Italian or French architect, and others even claim that it was King Parmar Dev of central India who originally built the Taj Mahal in 1196. However, all of these claims are easily disproved as there is written contemporary evidence of its construction.

Some people believe that the Taj Mahal should be enlisted as a new Wonder of the World, and several petitions are going on for the tomb to be recognized as such by state officials. In 1983, the Taj Mahal was designated as a UNESCO World Heritage Site, and it is truly a jewel of the former Mughal Empire. Over 20,000 artisans worked under the supervision of the imperial architect, Ustad

Ahmad Lahori, and together, they built a unique monument dedicated to love.

Conclusion

It is as if Aurangzeb, the last strong ruler of the Mughal Empire, saw the end. He wrote letters to his sons just a few days before his death, and in them, he stated that there was no hope for the future. Even though it took much more time for the empire to finally dissolve, after the death of Aurangzeb, the powerful courtiers took his descendants under their control, creating the puppet emperors whose only role was to sit on the throne and pass their days investing in arts and entertainment.

However, it is astonishing to think about how the Mughal dynasty inspired awe and admiration in the people of India. Even when their time was up, and their power was almost non-existent, no one dared to take the empire in their own name. There always had to be a Mughal on the throne. They started as unwanted newcomers, foreigners who conquered a distant land. However, they became an ever-needed presence, without whose name the land would crumble.

Even the Europeans did not dare to officially dethrone the Mughal emperor. They had to create a different narrative for the diverse peoples of India in order to persuade them to give up on their traditions. Eventually, the British East India Company took charge and removed the feeble old Mughal emperor, who did nothing notable except enjoy poetry and music. Like a criminal, he was arrested, quickly tried, and then exiled. The empire was no more.

However, there is a hollow prestige of the word Mughal that remains. It is still associated with the rich and exotic cultures of a distant past. And it is not the memory of the Mughals that haunt us today and draw us closer to their world. It is all of the monuments, buildings, music, calligraphy, history, scripts, and biographies of those emperors that still survive. Whether one looks at the Hindustani language, the *Baburnama* and *Akbarnama,* the glorious gardens of India, the Red Fort, the Taj Mahal, or all the other cultural heritage sites that the Mughals left behind, one thing remains clear. They all stand witness to the power and greatness of one of the richest empires in history.

Part 2: The British Raj

A Captivating Guide to the British in India, Starting from the Indian Rebellion of 1857 to the Indian Independence Act of 1947

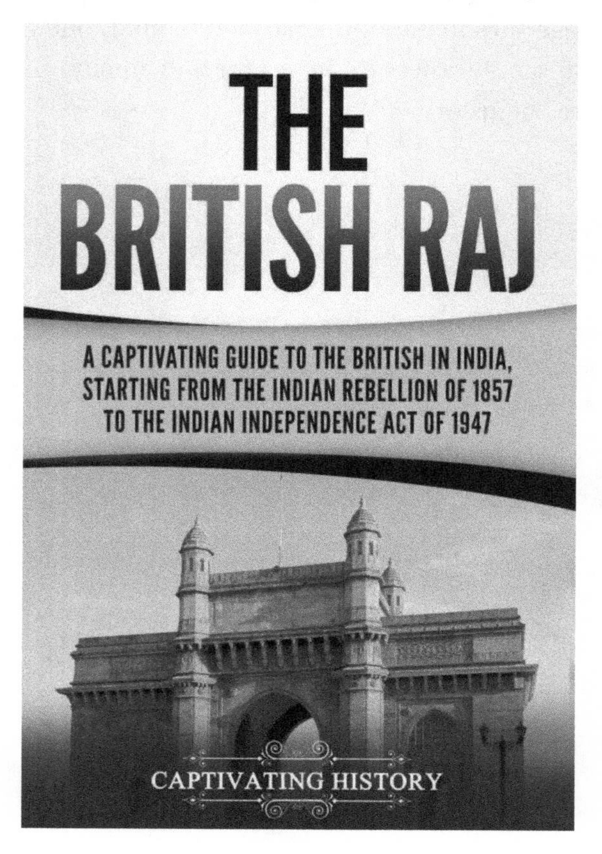

Introduction

The British presence in India lasted for nearly 350 years, but only the last 90 were under the direct rule of the British government. To some, ninety years might seem a short period to write a history book about. However, the time of the British Raj was very influential. It brought change to Indian politics, education, society, infrastructure, industry, and other aspects of Indian life. But while the British Empire brought modernization to its colonies, that modernization came with a price.

The British Raj did not cover just where India is today. In fact, it spanned across the territories of four separate states that exist today: Bangladesh, Pakistan, India, and Burma. It is estimated that around a quarter of a million British were buried in these territories since the East India Company set its first foothold. The oldest European graves can be found in port cities such as Madras or Bombay, where the first merchants settled trading offices.

The British spread across the whole subcontinent, starting as simple merchants who wanted a piece of the riches brought by trade monopolies in the East Indies. Driving off their competitors, the Portuguese and French, the British became conquerors, submitting all of India to their will. And when the political climate changed back in Britain, India was simply transferred to the Crown, as if it was a property that could be given away.

What the British government did, albeit unknowingly, is unite all the people of the subcontinent under one nation. Before the British Raj, the demographics of India were very diverse, with people grouped in smaller nations divided by different beliefs and cultures. But with the coming of the British, the need for unity grew and finally culminated in the late 19th century with the founding of the political party known as the Indian National Congress. Finally, the struggle for the independence of the subcontinent could begin.

One person rose as a star of the independence movement, and he became the symbol of the fight against oppression all over the world: Mahatma Gandhi. He inspired people such as Martin Luther King Jr. and Nelson Mandela. His philosophy of nonviolent resistance continues to be used even today whenever the common people of the world feel the need to voice their dissatisfaction with their governments. Mahatma Gandhi wasn't alone in his fight against the British. Various individuals, both Indians and foreigners, showed up to support the independence movement and drive off the British. Each had their own reasons, but they all had the same goal, even if it meant dividing India along the religious borders of Hinduism and Islam.

Chapter 1 – East India Company, the First British Presence on the Indian Subcontinent

The coat of arms of the East India Company

https://en.wikipedia.org/wiki/East_India_Company#/media/File:Coat_of_arms_of_the_East_India_Company.svg

The East India Company was founded by a group of merchants and politicians with the goal of sailing to the East Indies and establishing a foothold on trade. The desire of these merchants to travel and trade in these distant lands was no coincidence. The growing power of Spain and Portugal in the Indian Ocean was evident as the countries were growing richer. It was not that the British had never tried to set sail to the East before, but all of their efforts had failed due to the unpredictable climate of the unknown territories.

However, their luck changed in 1592 when the English captured a Portuguese ship that carried riches obtained from India. Among them were jewels, pearls, spices, and textiles. But one of the greatest treasures the captured ship carried was a manuscript with precisely drawn and described routes used by Portuguese merchants to reach Japan, India, and China. England finally had the means to safely reach these countries and challenge the Portuguese monopoly on trade in the East Indies.

Almost a century earlier, a Portuguese explorer named Vasco da Gama discovered a safe passage to the Indies via the Cape of Good Hope in Africa. Before that, the only known route was across the land, traversing Europe and West Asia. And even though the maritime route was dangerous since tropical storms were a frequent occurrence in Asia, it was still a much faster route, which enabled the quick transport of trade goods.

The idea of the East India Company was born much earlier among the merchant-explorers who were visionary enough to expand their area of business and profit to the distant lands. However, they had no means of financing such long and dangerous trips by themselves. They needed help and the inauguration of the Company by Queen Elizabeth I. By 1599, the Company gathered more than 200 merchants, artists, and explorers willing to commit to the trade in the East Indies. A petition was sent to the queen, but the cause was blocked by Parliament, who saw the Company as a potential cause of renewed conflict with Spain and Portugal. However, in 1600, Queen

Elizabeth I issued a charter in which she gave legitimacy to the Company, naming it "The Company of the Merchants of London Trading to the East Indies."

The first East India voyage happened in 1601 with the ship named the *Red Dragon*, which was commanded by Sir James Lancaster. The Company was successful in opening two free-trade zones, then known as "factories," one in Java, and another one in the Moluccas. The *Red Dragon* returned to England in 1603, and upon its arrival, the crew learned about the end of the war with Spain and the death of Queen Elizabeth I. Because the Company was successful in breaching the Portuguese monopoly in trade, Commander Lancaster was knighted by King James I, who recognized the value of new horizons that were opened to British trade.

The Foothold in India and the Expansion

It was during the rule of Mughal Emperor Jahangir (r. 1605–1627) that the Company first came to Bengal for trade. But the Mughals were not impressed by their intentions. The British had to endure a series of defeats at the hands of the Mughals before they were able to open their "factories" in India. Not only did the Mughals oppose the British trade in India, but the British Crown was also against the Company setting a foothold in the hostile Mughal Empire. Instead, King James sent a diplomatic mission to Jahangir with the task of negotiating and arranging a trade treaty.

The mission took four years to complete, and its success completely depended on the mood of the Mughal emperor and his fondness of the British diplomats. It was of no help that the Dutch already had a foothold in the empire and did their best to frustrate the efforts of British diplomacy. It was only when the British promised to bring goods from the European market directly to the emperor that progress was made. Jahangir was pleased with the terms, and in 1620, the first British factory was opened in Surat. Immediately, the British wanted to expand their influence across the

Indian subcontinent, but the unexpected high prices of traveling over the land stopped them.

A second factory was opened shortly after in Agra, but the spread of British influence was thwarted by the Portuguese presence in India. To achieve a monopoly on the trade in the East Indies, England had to conquer the Portuguese footholds on the subcontinent. The English and Portuguese were already in a conflict in Persia, where they fought over another trade monopoly, so the conquest of Bombay, Calcutta, and Madras in India is often seen as an extension of that conflict.

Madras was founded by the Company on the site of a fishing village called Madraspatnam, which was previously under Portuguese rule. This was where the British chose to build the Fort of St George in 1639 to defend British possessions from neighboring Portuguese settlements. The fort managed to attract local artisans, and it became a commercial success in just a few months.

Bombay fell in 1626 without much resistance, and the Portuguese retreated to Goa, but not for long. The Portuguese took it back shortly after, but because of the political marriage between the new British King Charles II and Portuguese Princess Catherine of Braganza, it became a part of her dowry. Seven years later, in 1668, the king gifted Bombay to the Company.

However, the history of Calcutta is far more complicated. In 1685, the East India Company requested permission to build a fortress on the banks of the Hooghly River that would protect their trade interests. Mughal Emperor Aurangzeb declined this request since he didn't want foreign fortresses built in his empire as they would represent a potential threat to him. However, the Company was determined to establish its authority in Bengal, and they used an army against the Mughals to prove their point.

The port at Chittagong was the first to fall, and the British established their currency there. The port city of Chittagong became the first city to be the property of the East India Company. The

British Army was supposed to move to Dhaka next, but the winds took them by mistake to Hooghly. There, the British soldiers molested the locals, which offended the Mughal leaders, who ordered the immediate closing of all the Company's factories in Bengal. The British realized then that they would never assert their authority in Bengal unless they built a fortress. But the Mughals still wouldn't allow it, and war became the only outcome. It would either end the Company's presence in Bengal, or it would result in some kind of permission for the British to build their needed fortress. The Company lost the war, and by 1690, they were expelled from Bengal. To retaliate, the Company settled in Madras and halted all of the Mughal ships that carried Muslim pilgrims to Mecca. Emperor Aurangzeb was enraged, and another conflict arose. This time, the British won, and they forced the Mughal emperor to admit them back in Bengal.

However, the Company was still denied its fortress. The British decided to ignore the prohibition and started building what was to be known as Fort William in Calcutta. It should be noted that Calcutta wasn't a city yet. Nobody knows what was previously occupying the area. The three nearby villages of Sutanuti, Kalikata, and Gobindapur were of no importance, and they were sold to the British. In their place, Calcutta was founded.

Back at home in England, the Company had to fight Parliament, which wasn't willing to allow the Company complete autonomy as the Crown would lose profits. The East India Company got its license renewed under the same status in 1712, and by then, 15 percent of the imports in England were brought from India by the Company. It was this income from India that ensured Britain would be the birthplace of the Industrial Revolution. The Seven Years' War (1756–1763), which was originally fought between Britain and France over the colonies of North America, increased the demand for Indian goods and raw materials that were used to sustain the army. Britain was in dire need of an efficient method of production, and thus, it became the leader in industrialization. As a result, the standard of living increased throughout the country. The demand for luxury goods from India only continued to increase as the demand back home grew. Soon, the East India Company became the single largest trade institution in the British global market.

The Seven Years' War wasn't only fought in the territories of North America. It also extended to the Indian subcontinent, as the French East India Company had an interest in the trade in the East. Britain was victorious on all fronts, which resulted in France limiting its ambitions for trade. The Industrial Revolution in France was halted by this defeat, as some of the Indian territories that were under their control were lost. Britain gained Pondicherry, Mahe, Karaikal, and Chandernagar. However, France was still present in India with a military force, which presented itself as a constant threat to the British East India Company, especially during the American Revolution, as British soldiers were often recalled to fight on another front.

It was the French Revolutionary Wars (1792–1802) that secured even more losses of French territories in India. Although France would remain present in the Indian subcontinent for the next 200 years, the trade interest of this European state would continue to steadily decline. The British East India Company virtually had no economic competition, but it would face revolts by the locals.

Modernization of India

In 1796, the British East India Company's governor-general started the reorganization of the Company's army. The Company had paid the native soldiers it employed well and gave them training in the European style of warfare ever since they were first introduced to the army. They were acquainted with modern weapons and the red coats of the British soldiers, and they were well-disciplined soldiers who willingly chose to fight for the Company because the pay was well beyond what the local rulers would pay and because it was regular work. Being a sepoy, which is what Indian soldiers serving under the British were called, was very popular, and the Company was able to afford a very large army. By 1806, the sepoys of the East India Company numbered 154,500, which made them one of the largest armies in the world. As the Company gained new territories, they needed to employ the local police. The police weren't as well trained as the army, but they were effective in dealing with issues regarding the Company on a local level. During the years, as even more territory was conquered, the Company had to transform the local police to local regiments. Garrisons were built, and depending on the location and need, it was filled with infantry or cavalry, sometimes even both. As the political picture on the Indian subcontinent changed, many armies of the local rulers joined the Company, obliged either by treaties, diplomatic efforts, or simply by conquest.

At first, the policy of the Company was to adjust the British people who served in India to the "Oriental" way of life. This means that the British generals and officers who served in India (most of them doing so their whole lives) had to learn the language and, for the most part, get used to the cultural differences between their European lives and the Indians. However, by 1813, the Company's politics had changed due to the influence of evangelical teachings back home.

At this point, the Company strived to use their Christian and Utilitarian philosophy to anglicize and modernize the people of India. The Christian missionaries started increasing their activity on the Indian subcontinent. The governor-general banned the Indian custom of *sati*, in which widows were burned alive on top of their husband's funeral pyre. The other changes the Company implemented also elevated the status of women in Indian society. The Company also strived to open schools for Indian children, which would teach them everything in the English language exclusively. However, the Company lacked the money for social projects and modernization on such a large scale.

Aside from banning *sati,* the Company's rule tried to help the position of women by rewarding people who married widows. However, for the conservative society of India, it wasn't enough for the British rulers to bring new laws to their country. They would often be disobeyed simply because they clashed with Indian customs and traditions. Even those who agreed to marry widows would soon abandon them. The men of India thought that nothing good could come out of a marriage with another man's wife, even if he was deceased. The Company's effort of reintroducing widows to society was mostly criticized by Brahmins, the highest caste in India and whose support the British relied on the most. The widows who were not burned after their husband's death were essentially condemned by the society in which they grew up. They were forced to step into the service of the British as housemaids, servants, or even lovers if they were still young and beautiful.

When it comes to the modernization of India, the Company invested only in those segments of life that would serve to increase its profits. The postal service was introduced to India in 1837, but it only connected the cities that were under the rule of the Company. Later, the postal service was expanded to the regions where the Company had its representatives, even if the Company had no direct control there. But the post offices it would open served all of the public, and any citizen could benefit from them. Although the Indian subcontinent had developed the courier service, the use of it was strictly limited to rulers and noblemen of higher classes.

By the mid-19th century, electricity was introduced to India, and with it, the Company brought telegraphy. However, in the beginning, telegraph services were only used for shipping-related businesses. Four telegraph offices were built along the Hooghly River to connect the line between Calcutta and Diamond Harbour. By 1855, the governor-general of India, Lord Dalhousie, was permitted to build 41 more offices and a line that would connect Calcutta to Agra, Agra to Bombay, Agra to Peshawar, and Bombay to Madras. This line would be expanded by 1857 to 62 offices. Telegraph services became public in 1855 and were available to everyone.

The railway was one of the services the Company needed the most, as trains would ship trade goods much faster from the production lines to the ports. However, even though the railway network connected the Isle of Britain by 1845, India posed a challenge with its uncommon and very diverse climate, monsoon seasons, lush vegetation, floods, and tropical storms in coastal areas. In 1849, it was decided to build three railways, which the British would observe and then decide if it was profitable enough to invest in connecting the whole Indian subcontinent. The first railway line to be completed was a 21-mile stretch that connected Bombay and Thane. It was completed in 1853, and from there, the railway network across India continued to grow. But railway construction was still very new, and India had no experts capable of building a large-scale system that would connect the whole subcontinent, so the engineers from England had to be brought in. This increased the price and time of the construction since the British experts had to get introduced to the land itself. By the end of the Company's rule in India, the railway network was only at its birth. But what the Company did was set the foundation for India to continue to build railways and go forward in the modernization of the subcontinent.

The First Conflicts

Robert Clive and Emperor Shah Allam

https://en.wikipedia.org/wiki/Treaty_of_Allahabad#/media/File:Shah_'Alam_conveying_the_grant_of_the_Diwani_to_Lord_Clive.jpg

During the expansion of its influence, the East India Company experienced constant resistance from the local rulers. The Battle of Plassey in 1757 is considered the beginning of British rule in India, as it was the first armed conflict against a local ruler, the nawab of Bengal, Siraj-ud-Daulah. He was allied with the French, with whom England had already fought the Seven Years' War. The Battle of Plassey is often seen as an extension of the Seven Years' War; however, it should be noted that the Company fought for its interests, not just for the Kingdom of Great Britain. France wanted a monopoly on trade in the East Indies too, and the French East India Company already had a foothold on the subcontinent and wanted to keep the British out. The British victory over the Nawab of Bengal and his French allies ensured that the trade monopoly belonged to the British East India Company. With Bengal firmly under its control, the British East India Company seized control of the entire Indian subcontinent over the next 100 years.

The British victory at the Battle of Plassey led to an estrangement between the Company and the Mughal Empire, as the nawab of Bengal, Siraj-ud-Daulah, was a Mughal ally. The cold relations between the empire and the Company led to the Battle of Buxar, which took place on October 22nd, 1764. The conflict was resolved by the Treaty of Allahabad, which was signed between Emperor Shah Alam II (r. 1760–1788 and 1788–1806) and Robert Clive of the East India Company and the first British governor of Bengal. This treaty marked the period of British political and constitutional rule of India, as the Mughal Empire gave the Company the right to collect the revenues throughout the empire. In return, the Company paid Shah Alam a yearly tribute, which the emperor used to maintain his royal court. Thus, the Mughal dominance of India came to an end.

Between 1775 and 1818, the British East India Company was at war with the Maratha Confederacy on three separate occasions. Maratha was an empire that was formed in the 17th century by the Marathi-speaking warrior people from the west of the Deccan Plateau. They were the ones who liberated most of the Indian subcontinent from the Mughal Empire. The First Anglo-Maratha War, which lasted from 1775 to 1782, was fought because the Company decided to meddle in the dynastic struggle of the empire. The Company won, and the outcome was the spread of the Company's influence over the territories of the Maratha Empire. Besides this, the Marathas were to prohibit the French East India Company from gaining a foothold in their territories, securing the monopoly of the British Company on trade in the East Indies.

The Second Anglo-Maratha War, which took place between 1803 and 1805, was fought due to the internal struggles in the Maratha Empire. At the time, the empire was a confederation led by five warlords who constantly engaged in internal conflicts. To protect its interests, the Company gave its support to Baji Rao II, the peshwa of the empire (somewhat similar to a prime minister), who agreed on a treaty that would doom the Maratha territories to submit to British rule. Not all of the warlords accepted the treaty, which led to the Second Anglo-Maratha War. All of the warlords eventually submitted, and the Maratha Empire became a client state to the British East India Company.

The Third Anglo-Maratha War, which lasted from 1817 to 1818, started because of a rebellion led by Peshwa Baji Rao II. Although he had allied with the British in the previous war, he was now unsatisfied with the Company's ever-growing power and the decline of his empire. However, the Company proved to be victorious, even though its army was significantly outnumbered. The Company had modern military technology and training, though, while the Marathas were stubborn in using their old ways of warfare. It was after the Third Anglo-Maratha War that the British East India Company gained control over the whole subcontinent. The Maratha Empire lost its independence, and it simply collapsed. Some of its territories were annexed and formed the Central Provinces of British India.

For the next three decades, the East India Company had full control over the entirety of India, and they profited greatly. They even took the opportunity to confiscate some of the colonies that had belonged to other European nations, such as the Islands of Réunion and Mauritius, which were French possessions. The Dutch Maluku Islands, better known as the Spice Islands, fell into British hands after the invasion. With them, the Company gained the riches that came with the production and trade in spices such as nutmeg and cloves. When Java fell to the British, the Dutch lost their foothold in the East Indies altogether.

Back home in the British Isles, the Protestant revival movement was growing. The Company was influenced by the movement, and it organized a systematic spreading of the religion throughout its colonies. Although the Company officially recognized and respected Hinduism and Islam in India, its members were very disrespectful of the social constructs, castes, and ethnic groups that belonged to them. It was the growth of tensions between the East India Company and the local religious and cultural groups, which would eventually spark a mutiny in 1824 and 1857.

The Barrackpore Mutiny

It was during the First Anglo-Burmese War that the order for a march of nearly 500 miles (800 kilometers) was sent to three regiments of the Bengal Native Infantry. They were to traverse the distance between Calcutta in Bengal to Chittagong (in today's Bangladesh), where they would be stationed in preparation for the front in Burma. However, this march presented several problems to the sepoys. Initially, the Burmese were victorious against the British, which led Indians to believe that their enemy had supernatural powers. As such, they were reluctant to fight against the Burmese. On top of that, these regiments had just finished a very long march from Mathura to Barrackpore, and they were tired and in need of rest and resupply.

But the alternative to the march to Chittagong was even worse to the sepoys. The sepoys were mostly recruited from the higher castes of Indians, and to them, crossing the water was a taboo. Taking a ship to their destination was sacrilege to them, and the British East India Company had to comply with their religious beliefs. This taboo is known as kala pani ("black water"), and Hindu people believed that if they crossed the waters to reach foreign lands, they would lose social respect and their cultural character. The only viable way to transport sepoys from one part of the country to another was by land. However, the railway network didn't reach all the parts of the subcontinent yet, and the sepoys had no choice but to march.

Another taboo among high-caste Indians required them to prepare their food and eat it from separate cooking utensils, which were usually made out of heavy brass. This meant that every soldier had his own heavy pack to carry during the march, making it even harder on them. Besides the pack, which contained food, utensils, blankets, and ammo, the sepoys were required to carry their muskets.

The sepoys demanded that the Company provide them with either bulls to pull their equipment and lessen the weight from the soldiers' backs or be paid extra money so they could buy the animals themselves. However, the Company declined the request of its soldiers, offering them the advice of discarding anything that was not necessary from their backpacks. The sepoys insisted on their demands because they could not break their own religious beliefs. That is when the Company chose to threaten the sepoys, declaring that if they did not stop complaining, they would be shipped to Chittagong by sea.

The sepoys wrote a petition to the commander-in-chief of India, Edward Paget, and patiently waited for the reply. When Paget heard about the situation in Barrackpore, he decided to personally deal with the matter and moved there from Calcutta. Paget was very conservative in his military ways, and the complaints of the sepoys sounded to him as a preparation for mutiny. He brought with him the European troops from Calcutta and ordered them to attack the disobeying regiments of the Bengal Native Infantry.

Depiction of General Edward Paget

https://upload.wikimedia.org/wikipedia/commons/d/d1/Sir_Edward_Paget_by_Martin_Archer_Shee_1810.jpg

The final order for the rebels to lay down their weapons was sent on November 2nd, 1824, but the commander-in-chief anticipated the refusal and had already organized the attack. The loyal army was sent to surround the encampment of the sepoys and wait for further orders. Paget ordered fire on the sepoys when he didn't receive any reply. In a panic, the sepoys tried to flee, but all the exits from the camp were blocked. The Europeans and Indian loyalists engaged in what can only be described as a massacre. Many bystanders, local people, women, and children were slaughtered during the operation. After the attack was over, an investigation concluded that the rebels had no violent intentions as they hadn't even bothered to load their muskets.

The leader of the rebelling sepoys was quickly tried and hanged. Those who didn't die during the massacre were arrested and then sentenced to many years of hard labor. Eleven more sepoys were singled out as probable leaders, and they were all convicted to death by hanging. The 47th Regiment of the Bengal Native Infantry was disbanded, and the Indian officers were all disgraced and weren't even seen as worthy enough to serve the government. All of the British officers who were in charge of the sepoy regiments, even though they could not deal with the mutiny, were moved to other regiments, where they continued their service as if nothing had happened.

It is generally believed that the sepoy protest was a peaceful one and that the British government of India used violence to suppress it. To preserve the image of the Company, no news agencies were allowed to report on the mutiny in Barrackpore in either Calcutta or London. The official statement was printed in the *Calcutta Gazette*, but it mentioned the rebellion as a trivial little uprising that was dealt with swiftly and without any casualties. The first criticism of the events happened six months later, in the *Oriental Herald*, which accused the British officers of slaughtering the sepoys. When other sepoys finally learned the truth about the incident, many deserted the

British Army. The general atmosphere of distrust between the Indian soldiers and their British officers was created, and it would eventually lead to the great rebellion of 1857 and the disassembly of the East India Company.

Chapter 2 – The Rebellion of 1857 and the Fall of the Company

A scene from the 1857 rebellion

https://en.wikipedia.org/wiki/File:Sepoy_Mutiny_1857.png

Prelude

For over thirty years, ever since the mutiny of 1824, the sepoys remained concerned about their religious rights during their servitude in the Bengal Native Infantry. The East India Company did nothing to persuade its Hindu and Muslim soldiers that their culture and religion would be respected. The Company continued the practice of recruiting from high-caste Indians and wealthy Muslim families, and both of these groups had their own concerns about their status in the army. Hindus still believed in kala pani, and they preferred to march instead of sail. But in 1856, the Company issued an act in which all new recruits were obliged to travel on the seas. Although the act didn't involve the sepoys who were already serving, they raised concerns about applying the act in the future. Their worries were amplified by the fact that the numbers of Christian evangelists in India kept rising. Soon, the rumor started that the Company was preparing to convert all Indians to Christianity.

The final drop for the sepoys was the introduction of new ammunition for the muskets. The ammo was packed in paper cartridges, which needed to be bitten off before it was used. In general, this wouldn't be a problem as long as the paper wasn't greased with what the sepoys presumed to be cow and pig tallow. For Hindus and Muslims, consuming these animals was strictly prohibited. Even putting the cartridges near their mouths was sacrilege for the religious sepoys. Soon, they started protesting, and it didn't matter that the Company promised the grease on the paper wasn't animal fat. The distrust toward the British officers was too great by this point, and when the Company announced a new model of cartridges that could be torn off, not bitten, the sepoys only believed that their previous fears were now justified.

As if it was some kind of curse, the birthplace of the rebellion that would bring down the Company happened to be the same place where the previous rebellion of 1824 happened. A sepoy named Mangal Pandey was angered by the disrespect shown to his religion and culture and wanted to do something about it. Many eyewitnesses claimed that Mangal Pandey was in some kind of religious trance when he fired at his sergeant major, who only wanted to calm Pandey down. The incident happened on March 29th, 1857, and the order to arrest Pandey was issued immediately, but no Indian sepoy would come near him. Seeing how he failed to inspire his comrades to mutiny, Mangal Pandey shot himself. But he only managed to wound himself, and he was arrested since he was now unable to put up a resistance.

As if it was a collective mutiny, the whole 34th Regiment, to which Pandey belonged, was dismissed and dishonored. Mangal Pandey was hanged for his actions on April 8th, 1857. The soldier who dared to arrest Mangal was promoted, but he didn't get to enjoy his new rank of sergeant as he was killed only six weeks after the death of Pandey. The culprits were the ex-members of the 34th Regiment of the Bengal Native Infantry.

Although Pandey didn't live to see the uprising, the story of his actions quickly spread through other regiments of the army. His death was the opening act of what would become the Indian Rebellion of 1857. He became not just the role model of the later rebel leaders, but he was also lifted to the position of a national hero. The modern Indian nationalist party often portrays Mangal Pandey as a mastermind who sacrificed himself to start the revolt against the East India Company, even though he claimed during the trial that he was under the influence of opium and couldn't even remember his actions.

Soon, the unrest started spreading. In April, Agra, Allahabad, and Ambala were burning. The sepoys did not openly rebel yet, but they were resorting to arson in protest over the cartridges and the general treatment of their cultures and religions. On April 24th, in Meerut, one of the biggest unrests occurred. The sepoys there refused to use the new cartridges during the firing drill, and as a punishment, they were all arrested. Eighty-five Indian soldiers were sentenced to ten years of imprisonment and hard labor. But the actions of the British officers were what caused the unrest the next day. They chose to publicly strip the sepoys of their uniforms to humiliate them in front of other regiments. Instead of provoking fear in the remaining soldiers, the British only managed to instigate their anger.

Meerut was also home to a very large British force, which had over 2,000 British soldiers serving there. The next day, it was the British soldiers who suffered, as the remaining sepoys demanded revenge. The Indian soldiers planned to release their comrades by any means necessary, and the revolt was led by the 3rd Cavalry. It was the European junior officers that were killed first, as they tried to stop the mutiny early. The superior officers were warned about the possible revolt, but they decided to do nothing as it was Sunday, a day for rest and reflection. Civilian quarters were also attacked, and a few women and children were killed. Off-duty soldiers who found themselves in the city bazaar were attacked by angry mobs, as the revolt began to be supported by the Indian civilians who supported sepoys. Some servants and Indian civilians helped the British officers by moving them out of the streets, but once they made sure the Europeans were safe, they joined the protesters on the streets of Meerut. Some sepoys showed similar care for the trusted British officers, women, and children, who were escorted to safety during the mutiny.

Rebelling sepoys moved from Meerut to Delhi, which was only forty miles away. There, on May 11th, they appealed to Bahadur Shah (1837–1857), the last Mughal emperor, to lead them. However, Bahadur Shah was an emperor in name only, as his rule was limited just to the city of Delhi. He was a puppet emperor who served the East India Company, and for it, he received a pension to maintain his status and court. He was content with his position as a puppet emperor, and he ignored the sepoys who called on him. However, Bahadur Shah's court abandoned him and joined the revolt, thus forcing the old emperor to acknowledge the rebellion.

Delhi had a large depot of ammunition and weapons, and fearing that the rebelling sepoys would get their hands on it, the British officers ordered an attack. In a panic, they killed their own guards who were stationed to protect the arsenal of Delhi. The sepoys were too many, though, and they kept coming at the British soldiers. Seeing that it was impossible to protect the arsenal from the rebels, the British decided to blow it up. The blast was massive, killing many civilians on the streets. This massive explosion and killing of civilians angered the rest of the sepoys, who had been reluctant to join the rebellion. The ranks of the rebels started swelling even more as a result.

Many Europeans fled the city in their carriages or on foot. Some were helped by loyal Indian servants or villagers, but many were killed trying to reach Meerut. Most of the Europeans in Delhi were civilians, merchants, and engineers of the British Empire, and they had been living in India together with their wives and children. Unfortunately, they were in the middle of the conflict and became one of the first victims. As if that wasn't enough, Bahadur Shah ordered all Europeans who were imprisoned during the unrest and those found hiding in Delhi to be executed in the courtyard of the palace.

Once Delhi fell, the reaction of the British officers led to many more sepoys joining the rebellion. A small number of Brits trusted the sepoys that they commanded, but many more tried to contain and disarm their soldiers to prevent the mutiny from spreading. This only instigated sepoys into open rebellion against their commanders. The military and civilian administrators were quick to remove themselves from the cities and take their families to safety. This was seen as abandonment by many loyal Indian soldiers, who then decided to join the rebellion. However, Muslim soldiers were not sure how to react. They didn't have the same resentment for their British officers as the Hindus, and the Islamic religious leaders couldn't agree on whether to proclaim jihad or not. Although some

Muslim soldiers took up arms against the British, a large number of them remained loyal to the Company and offered their support against the sepoys.

The Revolt

The Mughal rulers lost their power over the northern parts of the Indian subcontinent once the British East India Company conquered their lands. However, their name still resonated strongly among the Indian people, both commoners and nobility. The Mughals even evoked the feeling of respect among foreign leaders. As the sepoys had no Indian officers to lead them, the natural choice was their old emperor, who enjoyed his pension paid by the Company. Some historians believe that Bahadur Shah was stubborn and didn't want to join the rebellion until he was openly threatened by his people and the nobility of his court. The first thing Bahadur Shah did once he was officially proclaimed the emperor of India was to issue his own coinage to assert his new power. However, this proclamation of the Mughal emperor as an Indian leader turned the Sikhs and the state of Punjab away from rebellion, and they offered their support to the British to avoid returning to Islamic rule.

During the first conflicts with the British, the Indian forces were able to push forward and take some of the strategically important towns in the provinces of Haryana and Bihar, as well as the Central and United Provinces of Agra and Oudh. However, the sepoy mutineers lacked a centralized command, as their emperor was that only in name. Bahadur Shah was too old (he was in his eighties), and his sons, the princes, and nobility lacked the knowledge of warfare. Some of the sepoys showed a natural predisposition for leadership, and later, the emperor officially proclaimed them commanders-in-chief. One such man was Bakht Khan, who replaced the emperor's son, Mirza Mughal, when he proved to be an inefficient leader

The sepoys weren't the only ones who resented the British rule in India. The agricultural societies of some provinces rose into a civil rebellion because of the unjust treatment by the British. Because of the uprising of the Indian soldiers, the civilians felt brave enough to start opposing the British administration, which had given the Company unlimited rights over the land, leaving the peasants in perpetual poverty. The civilian revolutionaries were large in number, and that number only multiplied once they opened the British prisons and released all the Indian people who had been condemned by the British. Even though the revolt started as a military mutiny, it grew to become an uprising of the general populace.

The rebels felt the need for some kind of institutional entity that would provide them legitimacy and secure the territories that had been newly taken from the British. The emperor was just a symbol after all and was not at all capable of leading the state. A council was formed to deal with all the legislative and administrative matters, but the Company organized its counterattack soon enough, and it stopped all the efforts of the rebels to further organize and build a new state.

It didn't help that the rebels couldn't agree on their plans for the future. They did not share the same political perspective, and because of the many disagreements that arose, they were unable to bring to life a new political order. The Company even admitted later that India would have been lost to Britain if only one able leader had risen from the ranks of the rebels. The rebels were united only by their common hatred for the British rule, and this hatred wasn't enough. Each group of rebels fought for their own reasons, and the communication between the leaders was almost nonexistent. In some areas, the rebels were completely unaware of the fights won and lost in the neighboring provinces. But they did show remarkable courage, dedication, and commitment, and they managed to bring the Company to its knees.

Depiction of the siege of Delhi

https://upload.wikimedia.org/wikipedia/commons/4/47/Capture_of_Delhi%2C_1857.jpg

Having their military ranks significantly reduced (it is estimated that half of the total number of the Company's army joined the rebellion), the British sent for help. Due to the loss of loyal sepoys, they were very slow at organizing their counterattack. They waited for the British troops to arrive from either home or other colonies, which took months. Some soldiers were sent by sea, while others had to cross Persia because they had been fighting the Crimean War with the Russians (1853-1856). It took the Company two months to organize their field forces and start a counterattack. Two columns from Meerut and Shimla were sent on a march to Delhi. On their way, they killed many Indians, disregarding whether they belonged to the rebels or not. The British forces met at Karnal, and joined by contractors from the Kingdom of Nepal, they fought the main rebel army at the Battle of Badli-ki-Serai on June 8th, 1857.

The numbers of the rebel army remain a mystery. In some contemporary works, the strength of the rebels was estimated to be 30,000; however, modern historians believe this number to be an exaggeration. The realistic numbers are somewhere between 4,000 and 9,000. However, the rebels didn't have many firearms, as they relied on what they could capture from the British. Their numbers were largely bolstered by the civilians, who fought with swords, hooks, and pitchforks.

Although the British Army was greatly outnumbered by the sepoys and the civilians who joined them, the tactics they used brought them victory. The British were able to capture the gun stations in the villages surrounding Delhi, as the scared sepoys retreated. They ran to Delhi, bringing the news of the British Army being on its way. This news scared most of the civilians, who then abandoned the rebellion. But the British Army was tired, as the newly arrived soldiers from Britain and Crimea weren't accustomed to the climate of the Indian subcontinent. They suffered from both exhaustion and diseases, and they were in no condition to attack Delhi. Instead, they opted to lay siege.

Even when the British were finally ready to order the attack, the disorganization of the communication network led to confusion. The order demanded an attack on the city by the morning of July 14th, but it didn't reach all the officers in time. The attack had to be called off, and the siege continued. This confusion gave the rebels much-needed time, as their reinforcement from other provinces had finally arrived. The rebels from within the city attacked the British soldiers on two separate occasions and were very close to driving them off. However, the rebels continued to retreat at crucial points of the battle, achieving little.

In the meantime, the British ranks were decimated as cholera spread throughout their ranks. Even the officers succumbed to this disease and had to be replaced by less competent soldiers of lower ranks. Archdale Wilson was promoted to the rank of general due to this, but he did nothing to improve the conditions for his soldiers. It was the perfect time for the rebels to strike, but they had troubles of their own. Previous failures had demoralized the sepoys, and they refused to attack. The British finally received the help they needed with the arrival of the Punjab forces. With them, the British had all the needed artillery to bring Delhi down.

Brigadier General John Nicholson organized the bombardment of the city. He constructed four batteries consisting of various types of guns. Gunfire was opened strategically to fool the rebels into thinking that the main attack would come from the east. But the British attacked from the north, breaching the wall of Delhi on September 14th, 1857. Soon, the infantry and the cavalry stormed the city.

The rebels lacked the gunpowder and ammunition to efficiently fight off the attacks, and the morale of the army went even lower. They lost some parts of the city before they gathered enough courage to defend what remained. At one point, the rebels even forced the British to retreat and find shelter at the Church of Saint James. Archdale Wilson wanted to call for a retreat, but John Nicholson, who was mortally wounded, threatened that he would shoot him if such an order was given. In the end, it was decided that the British and the Company's army should hold their position and secure the parts of the city that they had gained.

Now the British Army was demoralized, and they gave in to drinking the alcohol they had looted during the attack. The rebels were not in a better position, as they lacked food. Both sides were in a rough spot and did not have the strength to organize another attack. Eventually, Wilson tried to bring discipline back among his soldiers and ordered the destruction of the confiscated alcohol. With renewed strength, the British managed to capture the city arsenal on September 16th. In two days, they cleansed the city of any rebel forces and forced Emperor Bahadur Shah to flee. The Company declared victory on September 21st, and Delhi was once again in their hands. John Nicholson died the next day.

The city was looted by the British soldiers for the next four days. Even though their official loss numbered 1,817 soldiers, it is impossible to say how many sepoys or civilians lost their lives. The rebels who were not killed during the attack were captured and imprisoned. However, the cost of victory left the Company with no means to feed both their soldiers and their prisoners. The choice was easy for the British, who wanted revenge for their fallen comrades. All of their prisoners were killed without so much as a trial.

Bahadur Shah was found six miles from Delhi. Together with his sons, he was captured and brought back to Delhi, where he was promised mercy. However, no such promise was offered to his three sons, who were all killed. Their heads were presented to the Mughal emperor, which, according to contemporary sources, depressed him so much that he refused to eat.

Campaigns in Other Provinces

In Cawnpore (Kanpur), a rebellion was led by the peshwa of the Maratha Empire, Nana Saheb (although the Maratha Empire had officially ended, the ruler kept some degree of authority). There, the Europeans were besieged in an entrenchment to the south of the city. The British major general in Cawnpore was Sir Hugh Massy Wheeler, who relied on his prestige and ability to negotiate with Nana Saheb, as he was married to a high-caste Indian woman and was a well-respected veteran. He did almost nothing to secure his people or fortify their quarters. The Europeans managed to survive the siege for three weeks before they were forced to surrender to the rebels because of the lack of food. But they demanded safe passage to Allahabad, which was granted on June 27th, 1857. Nana Saheb even provided ships that would transport them. However, while preparing to board the ships, someone from the rebel forces accidentally shot his weapon, and the frightened British started shooting, making it impossible to prevent a massacre.

The rebels killed almost everyone; only four men survived and reached Allahabad. Around 206 women and children were taken as hostages. Initially, Nana Saheb wanted the prisoners alive, but as the Company's relief army closed in on his rebel group, he ordered them all to be killed. All but five of the sepoys refused to do it, and these five men entered Bibighar ("House of the Ladies"), where the prisoners were held, and there they massacred women and children. This event is remembered as the Bibighar massacre, which took place on July 15th, 1857. Of course, the massacre only angered the British. After the massacre, the British Army used the phrase "Remember Cawnpore!" before each battle, adopting it as their official war cry. The British commander of the relief army was perhaps even more ruthless than Nana Saheb. While on the march from Allahabad to Cawnpore, two weeks before the Bibighar massacre even happened, he ordered all the villages on their way to be burned and all the peasants killed. His actions only pushed the undecided and neutral Indian citizens and sepoys to join the rebellion.

The rebels also besieged Lucknow, where around 1,700 loyal Europeans and sepoys served the British commissioner. For three months, the rebels bombarded Lucknow, trying to breach its defenses and enter the garrison, but they were unsuccessful. By the end of the siege, there were only 650 British defenders left, together with around 500 civilians. On September 25th, help was sent from Cawnpore under the leadership of Sir Henry Havelock, but his column was very small, and although they defeated the rebels, they couldn't break the siege. Instead, they were forced to join the British garrison. In October, another relief army was sent to Lucknow, who finally managed to evacuate the besieged Europeans. They decided to withdraw and not engage the rebels in an open battle, as they had a large number of women and children under their protection. They retreated to Cawnpore, and the rebels tried to retake the city. The Second Battle of Cawnpore took place on December 5th, 1857, in which the British won and thwarted the rebels' endeavors to recapture both Cawnpore and Lucknow.

In Bihar, the rebellion was mainly contained in one region, with smaller plunders and raids happening throughout the state. One of the bigger conflicts in the area started on July 25th in the Davanpur garrison. There, the sepoys of the Bengal Native Infantry planned to besiege the city of Arrah. However, the Europeans who inhabited that city were anticipating the mutiny and had not been lying idle. They chose the house of Richard Vicars Boyle, an engineer in the employment of the Company, as the safest place, and they built barricades around it. Once the rebels came, they couldn't do much but lay siege to the house that hid the Europeans of the city. When the British heard about the trapped Europeans, they sent a relief army that managed to fight off the rebels and free their comrades.

Punjab had only limited rebel activities, as the mutineer sepoys didn't have the support of the civilians. The garrisons in Punjab also didn't have well-organized communication with each other, so if the mutiny erupted in one of the compounds, others wouldn't even hear about it, let alone join them. Most of the mutineers who rose against their superiors in Punjab simply left the garrisons and marched to Delhi to join the main rebel army.

Almost all of the Indian subcontinent experienced uprisings to some degree. Some were easily dealt with, as the rebels were cut off from their main army, while others were lost because the British were forced to abandon their posts. However, it wasn't only the Indian subcontinent that rose against British rule in 1857. Other British colonies with Indian populations experienced uprisings too. These were often referred to as copycat rebellions, and they mostly happened on the islands of Southeast Asia, known as the Straits Settlements. Trinidad also saw a minor uprising, but the British secured the situation there before it could escalate. The British penal settlements of Burma and Penang demanded boosted security when the unrest spread among the imprisoned Indians. However, a quick British reaction prevented the outbreak of a rebellion.

Queen Rani of Jhansi

The area of Central India (now parts of Madhya Pradesh and Rajasthan) consisted of 6 large and almost 150 smaller states. They were under the nominal rule of the Mughal and Maratha princes, but they were all administered by the East India Company. There, the opposition to the British rule was largely centered in the Jhansi state, where Rani Lakshmibai defied the British. The Europeans sought to annex this state using a policy known as the doctrine of lapse, which stated that the area governed by a prince would be absorbed if the ruler died without a male heir. Although Rani Lakshmibai and her husband, Gangadhar Rao Newalkar, had adopted a son, the British refused to recognize the young prince as the heir of Jhansi once Gangadhar Rao died, since he wasn't their biological child.

Queen Rani in her cavalry uniform

https://en.wikipedia.org/wiki/Rani_of_Jhansi#/media/File:Rani_of_jhansi.jpg

Rani Lakshmibai was the complete opposite of what the patriarchal society of India wanted females to be at that time. She was well educated, and besides her interests in reading and writing, she was also skillful in shooting, horsemanship, and close combat. Her childhood friends were prominent leaders of the rebellion against the British East India Company. The reason for Rani's unconventional education might be due to the loss of her mother at a young age. She was brought up among the men of the household while her father worked for the peshwa of the Bithoor district.

When the rebellion first broke out in Meerut, Rani didn't want to oppose the British rule, which had allowed her to raise an army for personal protection. However, she openly defied the British authorities when she organized a social gathering in the form of a ceremony for married women (Haldi Kumkum). The ceremony also served as an assurance to her subjects that the British were weak and that they could be easily defeated. In June of 1857, the 12th Bengal Native Infantry Regiment attacked the Star Fort of Jhansi, taking all its treasure and ammunition. Even though they promised the British soldiers that they wouldn't be hurt if they surrendered, the Indians killed them all. Although Rani claimed that she did not organize the mutiny, the British still thought she was responsible.

Only four days later, the rebels threatened Rani, and she was forced to give them enough money to secure their passage out of Jhansi. As she was still the official ruler, she did her duty and notified the British authorities of what had happened to her. Trusting her good intentions, the Company gave her the administrative power over Jhansi until the arrival of the British commander who would take up the rule.

In the meantime, one of the nephews of her deceased husband thought the opportunity had arisen to take over Jhansi, but he didn't expect Rani to be able to defend her kingdom. She gathered her private army and personally commanded the successful defense. However, it turns out the British commander wasn't actually coming. Secretly, the Company sent the armies of Orchha and Datia, their allies, to invade Jhansi and divide it between themselves. But Rani was determined to defend her kingdom once more, as she was unaware of the Company's plans to annex Jhansi.

The invaders were repelled, as Rani was a good leader and tactician. She kept Jhansi peaceful for the next six months, still waiting for the British to send their commander. As no word was coming, her advisors persuaded her to proclaim independence. The British finally arrived in March 1858, but the city was well defended and wouldn't allow them entrance. Rani was smart enough to spend her funds in opening up a foundry, which produced cannons. Her army was also bolstered by the sepoys who had abandoned their posts and wanted to join the rebellion.

The commander of the British Army, Hugh Rose, demanded the surrender of the city, threatening its destruction if his order was refused. But Rani wasn't scared, and she lifted the morale of her army with a speech in which she confirmed her intentions for Jhansi to be independent of British rule. The siege of the city started on March 23rd, 1858. The bombardment was very heavy, and even the help of Tatya Tope and his 20,000 rebels wasn't enough to beat the British. The city walls were breached on April 2nd, and once the British entered the city, the fighting on the streets began. The bravery and determination of the Indians were such that in two days, the British armies weren't able to secure even one district for themselves.

However, Rani decided that the resistance in the city was useless and that it would be wiser if she joined the forces of the main resistance of Nana Saheb and Tatya Tope. During the night, Rani escaped the city with her guards and joined the fellow resistance leaders in Kalpi. On May 22nd, the British attacked Kalpi, and Rani herself led the resistance forces. However, she was defeated and was once again forced to flee. This time, she was accompanied by the other leaders of the rebellion, and they fled to Gwalior. They joined the Indian forces there who occupied Gwalior Fort, and they proclaimed Nana Saheb to be the peshwa of the renewed, free Kingdom of Maratha. Rani was convinced that the British would follow them, and she tried to persuade her comrades to prepare the defenses of Gwalior, but they wouldn't listen. Rani was right, as Sir Hugh Rose led an attack on the city on June 16th.

Rani Lakshmibai tried to leave the area, but her way was blocked by the 8th King's Royal Irish Hussars, who killed 5,000 of her soldiers. According to eyewitnesses, Rani wore the uniform of a *sowar* (cavalryman) and engaged one of the Hussars in close combat. She was dismounted and wounded. Bleeding, she tried to kill the soldier by firing her gun at him, but she missed. The Hussar approached her and killed her with his rifle.

Tatya Tope fled to Rajputana once Gwalior was lost to the British. He was pursued by many British commanders, but he was able to raise large forces of rebels wherever he went. Even after the Revolt of 1857 was officially put down by the British, Tatya Tope continued to resist, fighting with his guerilla forces from the jungles. In the end, he, too, was captured, tried, and executed in 1859.

Once the British took Gwalior, Sir Hugh Rose wrote a report to the British command, and in it, he described Rani as one of the most beautiful and dangerous leaders of all the Indians. He also reported her burial with all the ceremonies, and he claimed he saw her bones and ashes. In India, Rani Lakshmibai is remembered as one of the greatest leaders of the rebellion. In the eyes of her nation, Rani lived and died for her country, and because of it, she was made into one of the greatest symbols of the fight against the British Raj.

The End of the Revolt

After Bahadur Shah, the last Mughal emperor, was captured, he was taken to Delhi, where he was tried. His trial lasted for over forty days, and over twenty witnesses came forward to claim that he was the main leader of the rebellion. The old emperor claimed he had no other choice as he was used by the sepoys. The 82-year-old emperor wasn't able to provide any real leadership to the rebellion, but he was tried as the primary perpetrator of the events of 1857. He was found guilty and sentenced to exile in Burma, as the Company had no power to execute an emperor. The last Mughal emperor died in exile in 1862 at the age of 87.

After the disaster of 1857, the Company's rule in India was seen as highly inadequate, and corruption rose in its ranks. In truth, since the 1700s, the East India Company served the British government in ruling India as a non-official part of the British Empire. With the victory over the Indian rebels, the British politicians quit supporting the Company's rule of India and convinced Queen Victoria to take the title of "Empress of India." Through the Company, the British government inserted itself into the governance of India, and the abolishment of the East India Company was expected.

British Parliament passed the Government of India Act on August 2nd, 1858. The act formally dissolved the Company, and all its functions were transferred to the British Crown. A few months later, Queen Victoria proclaimed that all the people of India would be treated as subjects of the British Crown. The British government kept the bureaucracy of the East India Company, but it made a major shift when it came to the treatment of the Indian people. The new administration started a reform of the Indian government in which they tried to integrate the natives of higher castes and ex-rulers of the annexed kingdoms into the government itself. They also stopped all endeavors of Westernizing India, which meant the Christianization of the continent ended. A decree of religious tolerance was passed, and the Indians were allowed to step into the military service once more.

The British Raj was a construct that had the purpose, at least in part, to preserve the traditions and social hierarchy in India. The Crown often used this as an excuse for its rule over India. An investigation was conducted that concluded that the Company's efforts to introduce the free market to the conservative Indian society sabotaged the peasants, who were left at the mercy of merchants and local rulers.

Also, the Company failed to communicate with the local rulers and the common people. According to the British government, this was the main reason why the rebellions had happened in the first place. To serve as intermediaries between the British rule and the people, a new middle class of Indians was created. They were to be educated in new Indian universities and have guaranteed positions within the newly reorganized Indian government.

Although the East India Company was no more, the impact it had not just on the Indian subcontinent but also on the whole British Empire cannot be denied. The revenues the Company brought to the Crown allowed the expansion of British influence throughout the whole world, and the consequences of the Company's rule over India were both positive and negative. Their poor treatment of the natives led to the revolts that inspired India's fight for independence, but the Company did make it possible for Britain to become the leader of the Industrial Revolution, which, in turn, brought prestige and authority to the Crown.

Although the British often observed Indian culture as uncivilized and savage, many individuals of British descent fought to preserve it and keep it alive among the people who were ruled by a foreign power. For example, the first governor-general of India, Warren Hastings, learned the Pakistani and Urdu languages. He collected ancient Sanskrit manuscripts to preserve them, and he even hired locals to translate these manuscripts in English so he could make them available to the English-speaking world.

Chapter 3 – The Crown's Rule of India

The British Crown ruled the Indian subcontinent from 1858 after the East India Company was dissolved until 1947 when India gained its independence. The rule of Britain over India is better known as the British Raj. In both Sanskrit and Hindustani, "raj" means government or rule. Even though Queen Victoria proclaimed herself the empress of India in 1876, the British rule of the subcontinent was never officially named the Indian Empire.

It is important to make a difference between what we call India today and British India. The British Raj oversaw present-day India, Pakistan, and Bangladesh. Some places that are now under Indian control used to be the colonies of other European countries, like Goa, which was under Portuguese rule, and Pondicherry, which belonged to France. As Britain won and lost wars, other territories were included or excluded from the British Raj, such as Burma, British Somaliland, and Singapore.

The Crown rule of India was divided based on the type of territory. There were two types, British India and the princely states. British India was under direct British rule, while the princely states were ruled by the native rulers who were under British suzerainty.

There were over 175 princely states, while British India was divided into provinces. The biggest difference between the provinces and the princely states was in their courts of law. While British India relied on laws that came from the British Parliament and the legislative power of the governor of India, some states were labeled as princely states, and they were still ruled by Indian royalty. The rulers of these vassal states had varying degrees of freedom, depending on their size and importance. Whatever aspects of the government they administered independently, communication and defense were always under British control.

Queen Victoria often used her title of the empress of India in her speeches and propaganda material, and she even started two orders of knighthood that were special to India: the senior "Most Exalted Order of the Star of India" in 1861 and the junior "Most Eminent Order of the Indian Empire" in 1878. The senior order stopped new appointments in 1947. The last member of the order, the maharaja of Alwar, died in 2009, and the order became inoperative. The junior order ceased to exist with the death of the maharaja of Dhrangadhra.

The Government

When the Indian Rebellion of 1857 was over, and after the Company was dismantled, the British Crown issued the Government of India Act. This led to a series of changes in how the subcontinent was governed from that point onward.

In London, a government department known as the India Office was opened in 1858. It was an executive branch of Britain's government, alongside the Foreign Office, the Colonial Office, the Home Office, and the War Office. The secretary of India had the assistance of the Council of India, whose members were chosen based on the years they had served in India. No person was allowed to join the council unless he spent at least ten years in India serving the Crown's interests. The civil servants who were employed in the India Office were organized into departments, a system taken directly from the administration of the East India Company. All the executive functions of the Company were now transferred to the secretary of India. He was in charge of superintendence, direction, and control of the provincial administrations in South Asia. However, the decisions made by the secretary were executed by the provincial viceroys and governors whose cabinets were in India. The British government maintained a tight grasp on the government of India; however, after the First World War, that grasp relaxed, allowing the local government to execute its own authority.

The India Office did not govern only the British Raj. In fact, under its control were all the British territories in Asia, Africa, and the Middle East. At different periods, it would also take control of the governing separate political entities of Bengal, Afghanistan, Zanzibar, Malaya, China, Japan, and others. It also regulated the interests of Indian migrants to the West Indies, Africa, and Fiji. In reality, the India Office continued to be what the East India Company once was. However, instead of sharing its profits made in the East Indies with the Crown, it was completely subjected to the Crown.

The secretary of India was a minister of the British Cabinet and the political head directly responsible for the governance of the British Raj. As the members of the East India Company already had the necessary experience in governing India, it was only natural to install them as the clerks who would serve the new office. Lord Edward Henry Stanley, who was the head of the board of the Company, took charge of the India Office. However, this branch was divided into two departments in 1937. One was tasked with governing the British Raj, and the other oversaw Aden (in today's Yemen) and Burma, though Lord Stanley maintained authority over both departments. In total, 27 individuals served as the secretary of India between 1858 and 1947, the year when India gained independence and the India Office was abolished. The next year,

Burma followed the footsteps of the Indians and fought for its independence, making its office in London obsolete.

The Company had a governor-general office in Calcutta, and when the British Raj took over the rule, this position remained. However, the governor-general was now responsible to the secretary of India and, through him, to the British Parliament. This system of double government, one in London and one in Calcutta, had already existed under the rule of the East India Company, which had its Board of Control instead of the India Office. However, the upcoming years, which were the years of post-revolt reconstruction, brought changes to the Indian government. Before this, the governor-general had to consult the advisory council. Viceroy Lord Canning instead proposed that each member of the council should only deal with the tasks assigned to him. The collective decision-making route the Company had taken in the past was time-consuming and ineffective. The creation of separate departments for each of the counselors resulted in faster solutions to the pressing matters of the state. All the routine tasks of the government could be solved by the council members, but only the important issues needed the approval of the governor-general. However, the Executive Council still had the right to collectively decide what to do if the governor-general was absent. This innovation in the governance of India was decreed in 1861 in the Indian Councils Act.

The Executive Council could be expanded with the addition of a Legislative Council if the government of India needed to enact new laws. An additional twelve members would be added, and they would only be appointed for two years. Six of the new members were always chosen among the British officials, and they were the ones who had the right to vote when passing a new law. The other six were of Indian descent, and they only served as advisors. However, all the laws that the Legislative Council wanted to pass needed final approval by the secretary of India in London.

Even though the six members who were of Indian origin were added as a way to integrate the locals into the government of India, they were always chosen from a small pool of high-caste loyalists, and they were far from being the representatives of the will of the people. However, the true intention behind employing Indian representatives in the government was to change public opinion. These men were supposed to help appease the critiques of the government, both in Indian and British press, as their articles directly influenced public opinion.

In 1937, the Council of India was abolished and replaced with a similar council in London. This council had between eight and twelve members, and their task was to advise the secretary of India directly. All the members had to have served previously in India for at least ten years, and they had to have quit their offices in India no more than two years prior. The governor-general had the task of representing the Crown's interests in dealing with the princely states. However, in 1937, this task required a new department, and a new representative of the Crown was named. The Executive Council in India also had to be expanded to fourteen members by the time of the Second World War, with several new offices being founded.

The Indian Legislature consisted of an upper house and a lower house that represented the state council and the legislative assembly, respectively. The head of the upper house was the governor-general and the viceroy, while the assembly of the upper house was led by a president who would be elected for that position. The Council of State had 58 members in total, while the Legislative Assembly had 141 members. The president of the Legislative Assembly was appointed by the viceroy. This bicameral legislature had the power to make laws for everyone who resided in British India, no matter if they were of Indian or British descent. Also, the laws applied to the subjects of the British Raj who lived in other British colonies or the motherland.

With the Government of India Act of 1936, the new provinces of Sid and Orissa were created. A year later, the British Raj was divided into seventeen administrative territories, three of which were the Presidencies of Madras, Bombay, and Bengal. The other fourteen were known as the United Provinces, and they included the other provinces, including Punjab, Bihar, the Central Provinces and Berar, Orissa, Sind, and Delhi. All Presidencies and provinces were headed by a governor, and they all had their own legislatures. Each governor was a representative of the Crown and was assisted by ministers who were also the members of the provincial legislatures. All the actions of the provincial legislature had to be approved by the governor. The basic administrative units of the provinces were known as districts, and they were headed by a district magistrate. By 1947, the British Raj consisted of 230 districts in total.

Changes brought by the British Raj

Education

One of the most important changes the British Raj brought to India was in education. Thomas Macaulay, a member of the Council of India, spent four years reforming the education of the subcontinent based on the English model. He was the advocate of the Whig approach to historiography, which regarded the past as the progression toward liberty. He brought the ideas of the European Renaissance to India, such as the Scientific Revolution and the Enlightenment. Macaulay was dismissive toward the existing Indian culture, as he saw it as being inferior when compared to Western culture. In his view, the Indians were a stagnant nation that had fallen significantly behind the European scientific and philosophical ideas. He called his efforts at the reform of education the "civilizing mission." Some scholars today criticize Macaulay's "mission" as an excuse for the British rule to commit acts of racism since the government believed that Indians were not able to make any progress on their own and that they had to be ruled with an iron fist.

However, other scholars think that the British truly believed that it was their moral obligation to bring enlightenment to India.

The East India Company opened universities in Calcutta, Bombay, and Madras just before the Rebellion of 1857. However, it wasn't the Company who opened the first education center in India. In 1542, Saint Paul's College in Goa was opened by the European Jesuits, who also brought a printing press to the college so books could be spread easier throughout the subcontinent. The debate of the preferred language in which the classes of the new universities would be taught existed from the very beginning. The Orientalists thought that schools should teach in Indian languages, and they suggested either classical Sanskrit or Persian, which was the language of the Mughal courts. On the other side were the Anglicists, who wanted to introduce the English language in all schools in India, as modern India had nothing to teach their people.

The policy of introducing the English language in the education systems of the British colonies was enacted, and it is known as Macaulayism, named after its most prominent advocate. But this system only served the purpose of creating another layer in Indian society by introducing the class of anglicized Indians, who were nothing more than cultural intermediaries between the British and the Indians. The nationalist movement of India even blames Thomas Macaulay today for all the ills that came with colonization and for the creation of a new class that resents its heritage, and they strongly believe that it was the British people's way of imposing neocolonialism on India. Even today, the English language is used in Indian schools.

By 1911, the British government opened nearly 200 higher education facilities throughout India. They enrolled 36,000 pupils each year, of which 90 percent were men. After finishing university, the Indians were employed either in administrative services or as lawyers. This resulted in India having a well-educated professional state bureaucracy. However, the top civil service appointments were always reserved for the British who attended either Oxford or Cambridge. In 1939, the number of education facilities doubled, and the enrollment numbers jumped to 145,000 pupils per year. The Indian universities followed the curriculum set by Oxford and Cambridge, which meant they prioritized English literature and European history over India's.

Even though the British Raj opened many schools across India, literacy grew very slowly. At first, the British Raj only allowed higher education to Indians of high castes. Also, all education centers were concentrated in the bigger cities, with the countryside overlooked. In fact, before the 19th century, villages had their own educational institutions that taught their children useful skills, including reading and writing. However, the Company destroyed this system with its land control policies, and the village structure collapsed. India experienced an increase in literacy only after achieving independence in 1947. In modern times, especially in the period between 1991 and 2001, literacy in the subcontinent skyrocketed.

Agriculture and Industry

Some critics of the British rule of India would argue that the Crown was just an extension of the East India Company and that everything the British did in the territory of the continent was for their own gain. Even if this was true, it brought profits to India, as its GDP (gross domestic product) was raised to 57 percent, which was much better than the 27 percent achieved by the Company. However, the Indian population continuously grew, and the economic growth was not enough to boost the industry on its own, meaning some investments had to be made. To produce more, Indian agriculture had to be bolstered with a network of irrigation systems, the transportation of goods had to be improved, and Indian industries had to grow.

When it comes to agriculture, the British insisted on planting goods for export instead of food. Many fields were converted from food production to jute (a kind of fiber like hemp), cotton, sugarcane, coffee, tea, and opium. This conversion of food-growing fields into the production of raw materials, together with the Indian subcontinent's unpredictable climate, resulted in great famines. However, these exportable goods had the biggest impact on the growth of the national GDP. The demand for Indian raw materials was great, not just for the export industry but also for the domestic industry. India still had no competition in the textile industry since it produced the highest quality materials, which were always in high demand. Soon, the British realized they would have to expand the agricultural territories. But to turn territory into a fertile field, they needed to invest in irrigation systems.

By 1940, the British Raj had built many canals and irrigation systems in Uttar Pradesh, Bihar, Punjab, and Orissa. Many of these canals already existed due to the investments of the Mughal Empire, but they were badly maintained and needed modernization. The British extended the Ganges Canal, and it irrigated the territory of more than 350 miles. In Assam, the British cleared a jungle that occupied the territory of 1.62 hectares (4 acres), and it was converted into plantations, mainly for the production of tea.

Many of the irrigation systems that the British set into place served the purpose of watering the poppy plantations needed for the production of opium, which was mostly sold in China. The eastern and northern regions of India, namely the provinces of Behar, Rewa, and Oudh, were turned into poppy plantations. In 1850, the East India Company had poppy farms that occupied around 1,000 square kilometers (around 386 square miles). By 1900, the British Raj had doubled that number.

Besides canals and irrigation systems, the British Raj invested heavily in railways. The late 19th century saw the construction of a modern railway system that was renowned for its quality. It was also the fourth largest railway system in the world. The value of the railways lay in agriculture, military, and industry. The elaborate railway system ensured the safe and quick passage of raw materials to factories or ports, where the goods were shipped. The military used the railway for the quick transportation of troops and the movement of siege engines, weapons, and construction material needed for organized garrisons.

The funding for the railway system of India came from private British companies, and so, at first, private ownership of the railway was ensured. The Company first built the railway in 1832, and it was known as the Red Hill Railway. The British Raj expanded this network from an initial 32 kilometers (almost 20 miles) to 1,349 kilometers (a little over 838 miles) in 1860. By 1900, the railway network had grown to occupy a massive territory. During the British Raj, most of the construction of the railway was done by Indian companies, but the work was supervised by British engineers.

Both the First and Second World Wars crippled the Indian railway companies, as their production lines were converted into ammunition factories. A great number of trains were shipped to other colonies, depending on their needs. Without enough workers and facilities to produce both ammunition and railways, the tracks in some parts of India were stripped and shipped to the Middle East. The maintenance of the railroads was halted, and they quickly deteriorated.

Chapter 4 – The Famines of India

Victims of the famine of 1876–1878

https://en.wikipedia.org/wiki/File:India-famine-family-crop-420.jpg

Famines in India are a recurring thing, and they ravaged the subcontinent long before the British came. However, some of the most notorious famines happened during British rule, under both the East India Company and the British Raj. In the period between the 18th and early 20th centuries, around sixty million people died from starvation. It is believed that famines had such an impact on the population of India that they directly caused the long-term population growth in the subcontinent.

In India, to have a successful harvest, people had to rely on the summer monsoons, as they were responsible for filling the canals for irrigation with much-needed water. But droughts were not the only factor when it came to the great famines of India. The policies of the British Raj contributed to the worst famines that the Indian subcontinent ever saw. Many contemporary and modern critics blame the inactivity of the British government for the deaths of millions of people during the several famines that occurred between 1770 and 1943.

The British Raj adopted some of the policies developed by the East India Company, but many more were introduced under the Crown's rule of India. New war levies, rent taxes, a focus on exporting agricultural goods at the expense of food production, and the overall neglect of agricultural investments are some of the factors that directly influenced the severity of the famines in India. As stated above, the British economy relied on Indian goods, such as rice, indigo, cotton, jute, and opium. To increase the production of exported goods, millions of acres of land that had been used to bring domestic subsistence were displaced, leaving the Indians vulnerable to food shortages.

In 1866, a famine occurred in Odisha, and from there, it spread to Madras, Hyderabad, and Mysore, killing over a third of the population. Around 1,500 children were left orphaned, and the British offered three rupees per month to people who would take them in. The very next year, a famine in Rajasthan occurred, followed by Bengal (1873–1874), Deccan (1876–1878), and again in Madras, Hyderabad, Mysore, and Bombay (1876–1878). The famine forced people from these affected areas to migrate to those that had not been impacted yet. However, the bolstered number of people would cause another famine to break out, as there was simply not enough food to sustain them all.

The famines were followed by political controversy and discussions, which led to the foundation of the Indian Famine Commission that would later issue the Indian Famine Code. The code was developed in the 1880s after an extensive investigation was done after the Great Famine of 1876–78. The code was a famine scale, with three defined levels of food insecurity: near-scarcity, scarcity, and famine. If the crops failed for more than three years in a row, a scarcity level of food insecurity was proclaimed. Famine was defined both by crop failures and the increase of food prices to 140 percent above average. The famine level also included the migration of people due to a lack of food and heightened death tolls. The Indian Famine Codes were set to predict upcoming famines and therefore prevent them. Some of the policies of the Famine Codes included the rationing of food and the control of the food market during a possible outbreak.

In 1880, the Famine Commission concluded that each province of the British Raj had a surplus of food grains. The annual surplus, when added together, was 5.16 million metric tons. Bearing that in mind, the Commission came up with a series of policies that would regulate the response of the government to future famines. However, the governing viceroy of British Raj, Lord Robert Bulwer-Lytton, opposed any efforts to relieve the famine in India, as he believed the Indian workers would stop performing their duties, which would, in the end, result in the bankruptcy of India. He was strictly against government meddling in the reduction of food prices, and he even ordered district offices to discourage and disrupt any relief works that might happen. He referred to the Indian famines dismissively, saying, "Mere distress is not a sufficient reason for opening a relief work."

Previously, in 1874, famine had broken out in Bengal, and Sir Richard Temple, the lieutenant-governor of the region, successfully intervened. The mortality rate of this famine was very low, but Sir

Temple was criticized extensively by other British officials for spending too much money on famine relief. When Madras started being affected by a new famine only two years later, Lord Lytton did nothing to help ease the situation. This resulted in around five and a half million deaths, and Lytton was finally convinced to introduce a policy in which the financial surplus would be spent on relief efforts. Even though the measure was fairly lax, the British officials were satisfied, and they all complied with it. As one might be able to predict, another famine broke out, this time in 1896, and the measures were not enough to help the suffering people, as around 4.5 million people died of starvation. Unfortunately, it was as if the British rulers learned nothing. George Curzon, the viceroy of India between 1899 and 1905, continued to criticize any relief plans, and he considered the rations to be too high. His actions directly led to the deaths of millions of people, with some estimates as high as ten million.

The threat of famine was constant in India until 1902. There were no major famine outbreaks in India until 1943, which was when one of the most devastating famines in Bengal occurred. It took between 2.5 and 3 million lives. The Famine Commission identified that the cause of the famine was the lack of employment for agricultural workers. Therefore, a strategy was created to find work for these people. The Indian Famine Codes were used even after the independence of the Indians, and even more lessons were learned during the famine in 1966-67. The Indian government updated the codes and renamed them the Scarcity Manuals, which are still used today.

One of the criticisms of the government's handling of the famines in India came from a famous British nurse, Florence Nightingale, who pointed out that it wasn't the lack of food in a particular geographic area that caused the famine but rather the lack of transportation. She blamed the inadequate transportation of food on the complete absence of a political and social structure in India. She went further by identifying two types of famine: a grain famine and a money famine. The first one was caused by crop failures, but the other one was caused by the decisions the British government made while ruling India.

After all, the British had destroyed the structure of a traditional village in India. All land was now owned by the magnates, and the peasants had to rent the land they worked. This drained the money from the peasants to fill the pockets of the landowners, and it made it impossible for the peasants to afford food. Also, the money that should have been used to produce food was used for other purposes. Nightingale pointed out that the British Raj spent too much money on the military, and that same money should be put toward food production.

The same opinion was later voiced by Amartya Sen, the Nobel Prize winner of Economic Sciences in 1998. He, too, criticized the British government of India, blaming them for the inadequate transportation of food from unaffected areas to the areas undergoing famine. But it wasn't only the distribution of food that failed during the famines of the 1870s. The incorporation of grain into the grain market through the use of railways and telegraphs was almost nonexistent. The rails were already in place and managed well, but instead of the government using them to distribute the food to the affected areas, they were used by merchants, who transported their grain to facilities, allowing them to hoard the shipments. Telegraph lines were not used to communicate the reduction of the prices of grain on the market. Instead, they were used to coordinate the price increase, thus making the food unavailable to low-caste workers.

It was only after the Indian Famine Codes of 1880 that the railway started being used to transport the food surplus from an unaffected area to one that was experiencing famine. The Famine Commission also urged the government to expand the railway system inland. Up until that point, the main railway system was concentrated around important port cities that were used for exporting goods. The new lines were constructed, and they served the purpose of allowing food to flow to all regions that were affected by famine. However, even though the railroads ensured that food reached famine-affected areas, they could not ensure that hungry people would be able to actually buy the food. The Famine Commission relied on famine relief efforts provided by the government and did little to ensure the accessible prices of food on the market.

The railway system of India also served the purpose of transporting people from affected areas, sometimes even transporting them outside of India. The migrations, together with the famine relief efforts, was just enough to soften the blow of a mid-scale shortage of food. However, the migration brought new problems. Famine weakens a person's immune response, and many diseases, such as cholera, malaria, dysentery, and smallpox, took more lives than hunger itself. By migrating in search of food, people would bring these diseases to other areas, causing an epidemic. It was only after gaining its independence that India included the fight against infectious diseases in the Scarcity Manuals.

The Great Famine of 1876–78

The Madras Famine in 1877

https://en.wikipedia.org/wiki/Famine_in_India#/media/File:Madras_famine_1877.jpg

In 1876, a great famine occurred when the crops failed in the Deccan Plateau. The cause of this famine can be found in the particularly long drought that happened due to the interaction between El Niño and the Indian Ocean Dipole, which is when the western part of the Indian Ocean has higher surface temperatures than its eastern part. The result of this weather phenomenon was a widespread drought, not just in India but also in certain areas of China, South America, and Africa. As a consequence of the drought, a famine occurred, in which between nineteen and fifty million people died.

In India, the famine was severe mainly because the British Raj decided to continue with the export of grain as if nothing was happening. It is recorded that during the two years of the Great Famine, 320,000 tons of wheat were exported just to England alone. The viceroy who decided to continue with the export was, as one might suspect, Lord Robert Bulwer-Lytton. His tenure as a viceroy was largely seen as very productive, and so, the public often turned a blind eye to his ruthlessness in dealing with the Great Famine, as well as the Second Anglo-Afghan War (1878–1880).

During the famine of Bihar (1873–1874), a high death toll was avoided due to the imported rice from Burma. However, the government wasn't satisfied with the high expenses of the famine relief, and it was decided that the British Raj should lower its spending on welfare. The lieutenant-governor of Bengal, Sir Richard Temple, was the man responsible for the decision of importing rice, and during the Great Famine, he occupied the position of famine commissioner for the government of India. But because Temple had previously received strong criticism for his spending on famine relief, he was reluctant to do anything about the famine in 1876. During the Great Famine, Temple insisted that the government should not meddle in transactions done by private parties, and he also implemented strict standards for the eligibility to receive help during the famine. By his standards, only very small children, the extremely poor, and the elderly were eligible for charity during the famine, while everyone else was to be provided with "relief work." The work for able-bodied men, women, and children often meant relocation to the areas where labor workers were needed the most.

The measures that the British government undertook to relieve India of the Great Famine were not enough. In fact, they were so strict and inadequate that they inspired protests in Bombay. Those who were given "relief work" were paid less, and they were stationed in the relief camps near Madras and Bombay, living in very poor conditions. The payment of the relief workers usually came in the form of food, which would have been appreciated during the famine if it didn't consist of only one pound of grain and nothing else. Women and children received even less. If there was money involved for payments during the famine, men would earn one-sixteenth of a rupee, with women and children earning less.

Some people in the British government of India opposed these low wages for "relief work," and they demanded that the rations be increased and that some form of protein and vitamins be included in the meal, be it meat or vegetables. However, the reasoning behind the low wages was the belief that any excessive charity would lead to the Indian people becoming too dependent on government help and that the productivity of the workers would fall.

The pressure of the opposition did lead to an increase of relief, though, and protein was also added to the rations. But these new measures were implemented only in March 1877, which came too late for the many people who had already died of hunger. The fact that this government help came too late is also supported by statistics, which testify that, during the second year of the Great Famine, more people died of the malaria pandemic than from hunger itself. Even though a year earlier the famine commissioner had proclaimed that the famine was under control, the people continued to suffer and die throughout 1878, either directly from hunger or from the consequences of malnutrition.

The Bengal Famine of 1943

The Bengal province is mainly agricultural, with rice being the most important crop. In fact, the land of the Bengal province is covered with fields that produce a third of the rice that comes from India. Eighty percent of the arable land is covered in rice fields, which is also the main food for this region, next to fish. However, rice-rich Bengal continuously stagnated in food production while its population was growing. Soon enough, there was not enough food for both exportation and the locals. On top of that, the crops failed in 1942 during the peak of the Second World War.

According to the census from 1941, Bengal had approximately sixty million people living there. The growth in population is largely due to improved living standards and healthcare, which lowered the mortality rate. And even though the people of Bengal were mostly farmers, they produced the lowest amount of food in the world. This is due to the government's low investment in the area; thus, the Bengali people were forced to use underdeveloped agricultural equipment and the old methods of working the land. Of course, the government offered various types of credit to the people who owned the land or who were renting it; however, no peasant was able to afford a state loan that would help him develop his production.

With the rise of the population in Bengal, a need for more arable land arose. To acquire new land for food production, large forests had to be cut down. This caused the drainage of the soil, as the natural channels that supplied it with water were disrupted. New canals had to be constructed to replace the natural ones, and entire river flows had to be moved. But the government wasn't as interested in investing in the region as much as in exploiting it. Some deforestation projects ended up abandoned, and the demand for food could not be met.

By 1930, the Bengali region had transformed from one of the biggest exporters of rice to a region that needed to import food to sustain its population. On top of the shortage of food, there's some evidence that Bengalis ate the least nutritious food in India. The population mostly ate rice, which in those times wasn't enriched with macronutrients as it is today. The result was a malnourished populace who often suffered various infectious diseases due to the weak immune response of their bodies.

There is one more factor that influenced not only the start of the Bengal famine but also the efforts of its relief. The Bengal region saw railway construction during 1890, but that same construction led to changed river flows. In the 1940s, the areas that should have been naturally flooded were dry, and the fields that should have been dry experienced too much water. The changed river flows and the disruption of the irrigation systems due to the railway construction resulted in crop failures. However, the new railroad was mainly used for military purposes and not so much for food transport. The Bengali roads were in bad condition, as they were poorly maintained, and the British Raj mainly relied on river transportation to supply Bengal with much-needed food. However, the rivers were disrupted too much, and the food couldn't reach all the areas affected by the food shortage. The newly flooded areas were also particularly fertile grounds for waterborne infectious diseases like cholera and malaria, which additionally weakened the people of Bengal.

The already swollen population of Bengal was on the brink of economic disaster when the Japanese invaded Burma in 1942. Many people fleeing the war came to Bengal as refugees, placing additional stress on the region's agriculture and economy. Unfortunately, the Burmese refugees brought diseases such as smallpox and dysentery with them, resulting in thousands of deaths. Now, the already hungry population was facing a shortage of medicine as well.

Once Japan invaded Burma, the Bengal province became the first line of defense. The territory became flooded with military convoys, and the unskilled labor of the Bengalis was often used to build airports for the Allied forces that fought in the Second World War. The military needs strained the economy of the province even more, not just because of the great number of soldiers who came and needed to be fed but also because the locals were often displaced from their lands to work at military construction sites. Their land was often purchased for small amounts of money so it could be used for military camps, bases, and airports. This meant that a province that barely had enough food to sustain itself now lost the land that produced the food. The need for imports was growing, but there was no money to buy imported food, and there was also no means of fast and safe transportation for that food.

The province of Bengal was already facing famine when, in 1942, the government made a series of decisions that would directly lead to millions of deaths. The so-called "denial policy" was instated to deny the surplus of crops in certain provinces so the Japanese couldn't take it. Instead of distributing the surplus crops to the regions that faced famines, they were ordered to be destroyed. Later investigations showed that this policy increased corruption. The amount of food that was confiscated as surplus was far greater than it should have been, and instead of being destroyed as ordered, it was exported and sold for a much higher price. Another "denial policy" restricted the size of boats that were allowed to sail on the Bengali rivers. Any boat that could potentially carry more than ten individuals was destroyed. This meant that boats that would have been able to transport food were denied access to the Bengali rivers or were simply destroyed in fear of the invading Japanese.

However, on the local level, the provincial government started opening the gruel kitchens. At first, they didn't know how to react, and they delayed offering any relief to their famine-stricken citizens. In August 1943, the distribution of gruel started, but it didn't have enough nutritional value for survival. The grains served as food were often too old, moldy, and contaminated with pathogens that only caused new diseases to rise. Nevertheless, these gruel kitchens offered some hope and bought time for the government to react. Various national and international groups, such as communists, women's groups, merchant's guilds, and groups of citizens, sent donations of food, money, and clothes. However, they were simply not enough. Finally, in October of 1943, the new viceroy of Bengal, Archibald Wavell, brought military envoys that worked tirelessly on repairing the railroads and distributing the food to all parts of Bengal, no matter how remote they were. The food was brought from Punjab, which also sent medical relief teams. Thus, the healing of Bengal started. The very next season, Bengal had the largest rice yield ever harvested. But there were not enough survivors to collect the harvest, and the soldiers had to offer their help once more. But the work was far from over. Viceroy Wavell had much to do to protect the citizens of Bengal from going through the same suffering in the future. He made several political decisions that put pressure on Britain to increase the import of food to India. By January 1944, the famine in Bengal was officially over.

Chapter 5 – Nationalism in India

The Indian National Congress

In order to justify its government of India, Britain created a new middle class of well-educated Indians, whose employment in the government secured pro-Western and pro-British views of the local Indian population. They attended schools opened by the British government, and they were eager to get involved in politics with the goal of modernizing Indian legislation, economy, and society. After the Indian Rebellion of 1857, and throughout the 1860s and 1870s, the national awareness of the educated Indian middle class grew. It finally culminated in 1885 with the foundation of the Indian National Congress.

However, the educated Indians were well aware that they were under foreign rule and that they needed the help of British officials to be heard. Luckily, they had a retired British official named Allan Octavian Hume on their side. Together, they created an Indian National Union, which would work jointly with the British government. The Union had the task of being a mediator between the British government and the Indian people. They were the ones who made sure that the government heard the people's opinion.

With the British general elections coming up in 1885, the Indian National Union called upon the British people to give their votes to the candidates who best voiced their concerns about the social and political position of the Indians. They encouraged the people to vote against the taxation of Indians to finance British wars, and they gave their open support to the legislative reforms in India. However, the movement of the Indian National Union was a complete failure. The new Indian middle class finally realized that they could not expect the help of the British officials and that they had to fight their political battles alone.

So, on December 28th, 1885, the Indian National Congress was formed. Hume remained a supporter of the movement, which had now grown into a political party, and he assumed the position of general secretary. The first president of the party was Womesh Chunder Bonnerjee, an attorney from Calcutta. The first session of the new political party had 72 delegates in attendance, among them only two British members with the rest being Indians.

The Indian National Congress wasn't the first nationalist effort of the Indian people to have a say in the politics of the British government. There were many movements that came before the establishment of the political party, but they all lacked recognition. These nationalist campaigns had been mostly active in the political scene of India since 1875. For instance, the Indians protested cotton imports, as they wanted the textile industry to remain completely within India. The years of 1877 and 1878 saw the demand of Indianization of government services, as well as the opposition to the British efforts in Afghanistan. Many Indian presses supported the nationalist movements. In 1883, the *Indian Mirror* of Calcutta started its continuous campaign of promoting the need for an all-Indian political entity in the government. This campaign lasted until 1885 when the Indian National Congress was founded.

Among the first difficulties the Indian National Congress faced was the fact that Indians didn't have the same kind of unity that was generally observed in other nations around the world. This is because India was never really a nation; it was a mere geographical term for the territories of the subcontinent. The Indians had to be united, and they had to be given a national identity. They were a nation-in-the-making, a congress of hundreds of different races, cultures, and castes. The end goal of the Indian National Congress was the modernization of the Indian society. However, modernization doesn't equal Westernization. Even though the new middle class of India was pro-Western and had a British mindset, they were well aware that India was not a part of the Western world.

However, this attitude of the Indian National Congress instigated negative critique by some of the major religious groups of India. Muslims, traditional Hindus, and some religions practiced by the minority regarded the modernization of India as a breakaway from tradition and the "good old days." The past was often considered to be the golden age of the Indian subcontinent, and any attempt of modernization was regarded as Westernization and the promotion of the British culture.

Because India wasn't (and still isn't) a homogenous country, the political structure of the government and the methods used to get there had to be different. The Indian National Congress made a rule in the session of 1888 to not pass a resolution that was opposed by an overwhelming majority of Hindu or Muslim delegates. This rule was an attempt to reach out to the cultural and religious minorities in India. In 1889, the Indian National Congress added a minority clause to the resolution in which they demanded legislative reform. The clause stated that the percentage of Parsis, Christians, Muslims, or Hindus elected to the legislative council was not to be less than their proportion in the population.

The Indian National Congress created a common political program for all Indians. This meant that they would fight only for the rights and issues that were common to the native Indian population. The leaders of the political party understood that India was a multicultural subcontinent and that it would be an impossible battle if they were to fight for social reforms that would please every cultural group and sub-group that existed in India. This is why the Indian National Congress focused its political agenda on civil rights, administration, and the economy of India and its influence on the indigenous people of the subcontinent.

The Indian National Congress was made up of the educated middle class of India and had an elitist attitude. The leaders and members of the political party were often too concerned with how they would be accepted in the British government that they never really bothered to make their existence known to the common people of India. The political agenda of the party was also too concerned with more mundane political issues, such as the number of Indian representatives in the British Parliament and the freedom of speech for Indian politicians. While these issues were definitely important, other more pressing issues should have been addressed first, issues that affected everyone in India, such as the healthcare system, poverty, and the social oppression that the Indians suffered under the British Raj.

The Swadeshi Movement

In 1905, the British government decided to divide Bengal to raise the efficiency of its administration. Bengal was the largest province of India, and at that point, it had over 78 million people. The division separated the eastern and western parts of Bengal, but it wasn't just a territorial division. The Muslims in the east were now separated from their Hindu countrymen in the west. With the nationalist movement of India on the rise, the division was largely seen as an attempt of the British government to divide the singular country to rule it more effortlessly. They were afraid that the British rulers sought to turn the nations of India against each other.

The British government of India only wanted to achieve administrative efficiency with this division, but in turn, they created two separate nationalist movements in India that would continue to fight foreign rule throughout the decades to come. One was the Swadeshi movement of the Hindus, and the other one was the All-India Muslim League. However, even modern historians believe that the partition of Bengal had some political agenda behind it. Calcutta was the seat of the Indian National Congress, which had gained in popularity and presented a thorn to British politics in the subcontinent. In an attempt to displace the political party, the British government only managed to instigate nationalism in India, which would take the shape of terrorism, as the students opted for bombings and shootings to achieve their goals.

Before the partition of Bengal, the Indian National Congress started petitions against it but to no avail. A more aggressive approach was needed, and the Indian National Congress started calling all the people of India to boycott British products. The result of this call was unexpected, and the nationalist movement of India made a huge step forward by involving both rural and urban populations of Bengal into the state of politics. Suddenly, women and students started being politically active as well as the commoners. The nationalist movement of India grew from an elitist group to a popular crusade. The division of the nation managed what the Indian National Congress had been trying to achieve for decades, and the nation of India was finally united under a common goal, to oppose the foreign rule of Britain.

The Swadeshi movement took its name from Sanskrit, and it is nothing more than the conjugation of the words *Swa,* which means self or own, and *desh,* which means country. Therefore, Swadeshi means "one's own country." In the eyes of the members of the movement, Bengal was interpreted as the Goddess Kali, who had been abused by the British. In Hinduism, Kali is seen as the destroyer of evil, and as such, she was the patron goddess of many movements in India, whether they were religious, social, or political. Their rallying cry was "Vande Mataram," "Hail the mother(land)." The Swadeshi movement had the support of other regions of India, and protests supporting them were organized in Poona, Punjab, Bombay, Delhi, Kangra, Jammu, and Haridwar.

Officially, the Swadeshi movement was proclaimed on August 7th, 1905, in the meeting of the Indian National Congress in Calcutta. The movement gained political leadership and a more direct focus when the decision to boycott all British products was made. The leaders of the movement toured the country to spread the word of the boycott. In some places, they even gathered crowds of tens of thousands of people. As a result, Manchester cloth and Liverpool salt recorded a fall of sales by 5 to 15 percent in just the first year of the boycott.

In time, the Swadeshi movement would create a division inside the Indian National Congress, as part of the political party wanted to resort to more extreme measures, while the rest wanted to continue with their peaceful approach. In 1906, the Congress declared that their new goal was the self-government of India. In India, self-governance was known as Swaraj. The Indian National Congress was divided into Moderates, who were not ready for such a radical move as Swaraj, and the Extremists, who sought to speed up the process of creating an all-Indian government.

The boycott moved from refusing to buy, sell, and consume foreign products to an overall refusal of everything British, including schools, courts, titles, and government services. The goal was to make the administration of the Indian subcontinent impossible for the British government and to lessen the exploitation of the Indian territories, which only served to help British commerce. The British government saw the resignation of a large number of Indian officials, such as constables, deputies, clerks, and even sepoys. On the other hand, some of the members of the Swadeshi Movement opted for the use of violence to fight the British government. However, it was the boycott of the foreign goods that had the best results.

However, in 1908, the movement experienced a cooling phase. It ultimately failed, largely because it didn't manage to engage the

Muslim population, especially in the countryside. The British government observed the Swadeshi movement as a threat, and it came down on it with a heavy hand. To demotivate the movement, the government banned all public gatherings, processions, and press. Students who participated in the movement rallies were expelled from colleges, and the government officials who supported the movement were removed from their offices. People were often beaten up by the police, and they faced fines that were impossible for commoners to pay.

Even though the Swadeshi movement declined, it did bring up ideas that would only serve to reinforce Indian nationalism. The movement left its trail in the culture of India through literature, song, and storytelling, and these continued to spread throughout the Indian subcontinent, even though the movement achieved little to nothing. The Swadeshi movement was only the beginning of the Indian struggle against British colonialism, though. The ideas behind it would continue to exist, and it would be newly awakened in the future through the efforts of Mahatma Gandhi.

The All-India Muslim League

Just as with Hindus, the British Raj failed to incorporate Muslims and their teachings into the new social structure of India. Even though the Muslim educational centers were open, they focused on the British curriculum and sciences. This created a response from Muslim scholars, who advocated for Islamic teachings and who opposed the notion that all citizens of India, both Muslim and Hindu, had to be Westernized. The national identity of Muslims was indeed present much earlier than that of Hindus; however, their preoccupation with the preservation of their culture and religion diverted them from fully entering the political scene.

All-India Muslim League conference

https://upload.wikimedia.org/wikipedia/commons/7/74/All_India_Muslim_league_conference_1906_attendees_in_Dhaka.jpg

The efforts to preserve Muslim education, culture, and religion were impossible without certain special rights that needed to be obtained from the British government. The need for a separate political party was obvious, and some individuals among the Muslim scholars organized themselves into a political party known as the All-India Muslim League. The League was formed in Dhaka, Bangladesh, in December 1906. It was formed a year after the partition of Bengal occurred, as the event only sped up the creation of the League since it concentrated Muslims into the eastern territories of the province and elevated their sense of a separate nation.

The founder of the All-India Muslim League, Nawab Khwaja Salimullah, wasn't elected as its first president. The honor of that position belonged to another founder of the League, Sir Sultan Muhammad Shah (Aga Khan III). Both Salimullah and Muhammad Shah were patrons of Muslim education in India, and they both strongly believed that Muslims needed an educational capital before indulging in politics. They fought for the opening of a Muslim university in Dhaka, but it was not until 1911 that they would succeed. The annulment of the partition of Bengal by King George V was performed that year, and the All-Muslim League became even more concerned about the interests of Muslims in the area of education. It was only when they voiced their concerns after the reunification of Hindu and Muslim Bengal that they were granted permission to open a Muslim university in Dhaka.

One of the first things the All-India Muslim League demanded after its creation was separate representation in the British government, and their first victory toward this goal happened in 1908 when the House of Lords accepted their proposal. However, the League was unsatisfied with the number of seats that were to be reserved for Muslim representatives in Parliament. The very next year, Muslims protested the government's decision, and to make a compromise, more seats were given to Muslim representatives.

The Muslims and Hindus found a common language during World War I, as both groups had similar rights to fight for. There was even an attempt to form a Muslim-Hindu alliance; however, once the war ended, this alliance wouldn't live for long. The Muslims and Hindus grew apart, with each group turning back to their community. The Muslims were outraged that the Ottoman Empire had been placed under sanctions after World War I, and they organized riots across India that were meant to display their support to the Ottoman Empire. Many Muslim politicians even left their positions in the government. The All-India Muslim League recognized that the British "two-nations in one state" belief (that Muslims and Hindus could live together in one state) was impossible to maintain, and the League changed their agenda from advocating for Muslim rights within India to the creation of an all-Muslim state in the Indian subcontinent. The idea of Pakistan was born, but the British government strongly opposed it. For the British Raj, India had to be one political entity, not just because of the administration but also because of the economic gains. If Muslims had their own state, Britain would be forced to treat them as a separate economic entity as well.

During the 1940s, the All-India Muslim League grew, attracting over two million members. However, their political views became more and more influenced by religion. They could not see a reason to stay united with the Hindus, with whom they shared nothing in common. Their cultures, language, literature, and history were completely different, and as such, they believed that the two nations couldn't possibly live under the same government. The sentiment for separatism grew exponentially. However, not all Muslims felt this way. Some declared it would be best for all social groups to remain united under one state. When the All-India Muslim League passed the resolution to create a new state, they were opposed by other Muslim groups, such as the All India Azad Muslim Conference. The violent conflict was inevitable, and the leader of the Azad Muslim Conference, Allah Bakhsh Soomro, was murdered.

The new Muslim state of Pakistan would contain the provinces of Sindh, Punjab, Baluchistan, the Northwest Frontier Province, and Bengal. The declaration of the resolution of the All-India Muslim League led to even more violent conflicts, especially in the aforementioned provinces. Instead of suing for peace, the League financed their supporters, who rallied and protested, often creating unrest and committing violence against Hindus and Sikhs.

However, there was nothing the League could do to gain the support for Pakistan within the British government. Only after the British rule of India ended in 1947 could the new state be created. Even then, the League couldn't agree on the future of their new state, and it became divided into smaller political parties with different ideologies. Later, the All-India Muslim League would reunite, this time under a different name, the Pakistan Muslim League.

Chapter 6 – India during World War I

Indian bicycle troops at the Battle of the Somme

https://en.wikipedia.org/wiki/Indian_Army_during_World_War_I#/media/File:Indian_bicycle_troops_Somme_1916_IWM_Q_3983.jpg

The Ghadar Movement

Since 1904, the West Coast of North America had been an attractive migration destination for many Indians, especially those from the Punjab area. The hunger, poverty, and lack of opportunities forced Indians to seek employment in other states, and while the British government was satisfied to let the Indians work on their plantations in Fiji and Burma, they were against migration to North America, where socialist ideas of freedom were on the rise. By 1908, the secretary of state of India even implemented restrictions on immigration to Canada because he was afraid that if Indians met the free Western world, the British government would lose the prestige by which they ruled India. The British Raj did not need to use force during their rule over this issue, as Indians believed they were a part of a greater empire.

Despite the restrictions, some Indians managed to emigrate to Canada and the western states of the United States. They were veteran soldiers of the British Indian Army, and since they had fought around the world, they already knew of the prosperity of the Western world. Even though these men and their families faced harsh racism and scrutiny in the West, they chose to stay, as the poverty and hunger back home was the only other option. Shunned away from the predominantly white communities of Canada and America, Indians organized themselves into tight-knit groups, where they allowed their nationalistic ideas to grow. However, instead of fighting for their rights in the lands where they found themselves, they focused their efforts on the situation back home in India. They felt that as long as they were not free in India, they could not expect other nations to treat them as equals.

Various Indian nationalistic movements started popping up in the West, and they even organized newspapers that promoted their separatist ideas, such as *Circular-e-Azadi* in San Francisco or *Free Hindustan* in Vancouver. Indian immigrants remembered the Swadeshi movement, and they pledged their support to it. Some political exiles from India found their new homes in Canada and the US, where they continued to promote their ideas of overthrowing British rule. The first to preach a violent revolution against the British was a Sikh priest named Bhagwan Singh, who came to the West in 1913, just before the start of the First World War.

Bhagwan Singh was banished from Canada, and he moved to the US, where the political teachings of Lala Har Dayal had already gathered Indian immigrants into one community. Har Dayal was a professor at Stanford University, but his efforts to help immigrant workers in the US led him to politics. After the attempted assassination of Lord Charles Hardinge, the viceroy of India, in 1912, Har Dayal realized that there was a possibility for a revolutionary overthrow of the British government, and he moved his focus from workers' syndicates for immigrants in the US to the preaching of an armed and violent uprising in India. He founded the Hindi Association in Portland and started preaching to the immigrant Indians to go back home and call their countrymen to take up arms against the British. The ideas of Har Dayal were quickly accepted by the immigrants, and a new publication, the *Hindustan Ghadar*, was issued weekly, calling for revolution. As one might surmise, the Ghadar movement got its name from this publication.

The onset of World War I didn't stop the plans of the Ghadar movement. In fact, they saw it as an opportunity to plant the seeds of revolution among the Indian soldiers, who would, in turn, fight against the British instead of beside them. They spread their propaganda not just among the immigrants in the US and Canada but also to the Indians working in the Malay States, Fiji, the Philippines, China, and Japan, calling them to go back home and instigate a revolution.

But the Ghadar movement didn't keep their revolution a secret, which was a grave mistake. Instead of silently organizing the revolt back home, their propaganda was very loud, and it circulated the world. Once the movement was ready to take action, the British government in India was ready for them. The first immigrants who returned to Indian soil were apprehended. Those who were recognized as being less dangerous were confined to their villages under strict orders not to leave them. The more dangerous immigrants, though, were arrested. However, many Ghadar members managed to arrive in India undetected, and they proceeded to Punjab, where they planned to start their revolution.

Unfortunately for them, the Punjab they hoped to return to was different from what they expected. Even though the Ghadar movement propaganda had reached them, the citizens were passive and simply had no interest in revolution. The leaders of the movement tried their best to spark nationalism in their fellow Indians but to no avail. Some of the Punjab citizens started reporting the Ghadar leaders, which led to their arrests. Aware that they were being received with scorn, the Ghadars tried to spread their influence through the ranks of the sepoys. Although they were successful at instigating small-scale mutinies among the soldiers, they lacked centralized leadership, which would allow them to focus their efforts more clearly.

The leaders of the Ghadar movement had also just returned from spending many years in Canada, the US, and even Germany, which made them unpopular among the locals. They quickly became aware that they needed someone familiar, someone who already proved his worth to the territory of India, if they were to inspire the citizens. The very next year, in 1915, Rash Behari Bose answered their call and accepted the leadership of the Ghadar movement. Bose was already very popular among the Indians who were against colonial rule, as he was the one who had attempted the assassination of Viceroy Lord Charles Hardinge in 1912.

With this new leadership, the Ghadar movement improved their communication and organization. Bose sent men to various military garrisons with the task of spreading the word of the upcoming mutiny and recruiting willing sepoys. On February 11th, 1915, the scouts returned, bearing optimistic reports, and the Ghadar movement set the date of the uprising for February 21st. However, an agent of the Criminal Investigation Department managed to infiltrate the movement, and he notified the government of Bose's plans. The Ghadar members sensed something was up, and they decided to speed up the mutiny and move it to February 19th. However, the undercover agent was not caught, and he brought the new details to the government, which was more than ready to take action against the movement.

Most of the Ghadar leaders were arrested, although Bose managed to escape, and the mutiny was crushed even before it had started. The government wanted to set an example to prevent any future organizations attempting similar efforts as the Ghadar movement. Punjab and Mandalay (Burma) saw an excessive number of conspiracy trials that sentenced 45 revolutionaries to death, with over 200 sentenced to prison. The government's retaliation left India without an entire generation of nationalist leaders in Punjab.

However, the failure of the Ghadar movement didn't discourage all revolutionaries. Some still operated, especially the Indian migrants in Berlin and the US under the leadership of Ram Chandra. With the help of the German government, which was eager to dispose of British supremacy, they continued to make attempts to instigate mutinies. They succeeded in inspiring violent opposition to British rule, but it only took place in a few locations, and there were not enough numbers to start a widespread Indian revolt. Even though the Ghadar movement failed to make a significant political change in India, what it did do was keep the spirit of nationalism alive and remind civilians of the Swadesh ideology and that self-governance of India could be attained if enough people united.

The Home Rule Movement

In 1909, Bal Gangadhar Tilak, an Indian nationalist and independence activist, was exiled from India and sentenced to spend the next six years in a prison in Mandalay, Burma. He was accused of organizing protests and holding speeches against the British government on three separate occasions, in 1897, 1902, and later in 1916. Tilak was a member of the Indian National Congress, and he had belonged to the Extremists when the Congress split into two in 1907. In 1915, he was back in India, and he wanted to rejoin the Congress and mend the split between the Extremists and Moderates. To do so, he made a public declaration, in which he made a comparison between the Irish Home Rule movement and the nationalist Indians. Tilak believed that Indians should seek to reform the administrative system and not overthrow the government, which had happened in Ireland. He also publicly condemned all the violent attacks on the British that had happened under the influence of the Ghadar movement. He offered his full support to the British Crown, and he urged all Indians to offer their help to the government in the wake of World War I.

The Indian National Congress proved to be very sympathetic toward Tilak, especially because they were pressured by another important political character that vigorously worked on the reformation of India, Mrs. Annie Besant. She joined the Congress in 1914 and was keen to wake up the dormant party and push it to national political activity.

At the time, Annie Besant was 66 years old, but her political career had started back in England during her youth. She became aware of the situation of the poor in England after her marriage when she was twenty. Soon, she learned about the English radicals and the Union of Farmers, who demanded better working conditions. Besant clashed with her husband, who had different political ideas than her, and the couple split after only six years of marriage. She then enrolled in the Birkbeck Literary and Scientific Institution, which was where she started her activism work in the area of religion and politics. She was the most active in areas such as women's rights, birth control, secularism, socialism, and worker's rights. Besant actually shared her ideas with Irish writer George Bernard Shaw, with whom she grew very close to and possibly started a relationship. However, divorces were unavailable to a woman of middle-class status in 19th-century England, and she remained the legal wife of her previous husband, who condemned her love affair with the Irish writer. Besant started to show interest in the occult and became a member of the Theosophical Society. This occult society sought to make a connection between various religions, and it found inspiration in Hindu, Buddhism, and Sufi teachings, as well as in Christianity. It was this society that brought Annie Besant to India in 1893, where she became interested in the social problems of castes and foreign rule.

Once she joined the Indian National Congress in 1914, her attention switched from social activism to building a home rule similar to the Irish Home Rule movement. To do this, she needed the support of both the Extremists and Moderates, and she worked hard with Tilak on mending the wounds caused by the party split. They were successful, and the Congress reunited both factions into one political party. However, their success was partial, as the Moderates of the Bengal wing of the Indian National Congress did not allow the Extremists to rejoin their midst.

During 1915, Annie Besant launched a campaign in which she called for public meetings and conferences to demand the self-government of India. Her actions, and those of Tilak, changed the minds of the leaders of the Bengal wing of the Indian National Congress, and finally, the party was made whole again. However, Besant had no luck in attracting the Congress and the Muslim League to her idea of setting up a home rule. Tilak was attracted to her idea, though, and he took the initiative and set up his own home rule league in Bombay. Since the Indian National Congress remained passive regarding self-government, in September 1916, Besant left them to set up her home rule league, and she gained many followers. The two separate home rule leagues existed at the same time as each other, but they avoided conflicts by setting up in the territories in which they would be active. Tilak's league worked in the areas of Maharashtra, Karnataka, the Central Provinces, and Berar, while Annie's league operated throughout the rest of India.

The two leagues never merged, and although Besant claimed she had nothing against Tilak, some of his conservative convictions regarding the rights of Indian women may have kept them apart. Although Tilak had progressive beliefs when it came to the politics of India, he remained very conservative when it came to social reforms. He opposed the reforms that fought against untouchability, a practice that ostracizes minorities, in the caste system of India. He was also against raising the consent age for the marriage of girls, as he claimed it would break Hindu tradition. The consent age, according to Hindu tradition, was ten years, and the British government successfully raised it to twelve despite very strong opposition by the conservatives. However, Tilak had a great number of followers; by April 1917, his home rule league had 14,000 members.

In contrast to Tilak's league, Besant had only gathered 7,000 members by May 1917. Many of those members were followers of her Theosophical Society, and they remained inactive in Indian politics. However, Besant's strength wasn't in numbers but in the ideology she represented. While Tilak tried to make an excuse for caste differences, Besant's home league worked on setting up education centers and libraries for lower castes. She also actively worked on removing the concept of untouchability. Even though Annie Besant and Tilak had completely different views on the social status of Indians, they never publicly opposed each other since they had the same goal of promoting the self-government of India.

As both home rule leagues grew in popularity, spreading their influence through the universities of India, the British government had to react. In June 1917, Besant and her associates were arrested. However, the government didn't expect India to protest their internment so vigorously. A wave of nationwide anger toward the government's actions pushed some prominent Indians to renounce the British rule. Sir Subbier Subramania Iyar, a knight commander of the Most Eminent Order of the Indian Empire, renounced his knighthood in protest. Even those Congress members who hesitated to join the home rule movement did so at this point. Tilak called upon civilians to engage in civil disobedience until Besant and her associates were released from their imprisonment.

The unrest caused by the imprisonment of Annie Besant was effective on two fronts. She was released in September of 1917, and the new secretary of state of India, Edwin Montagu, made a historic declaration on August 20th, 1917. He stated that the new policy of employing more Indians in the government's administration was to be immediately put in effect in preparation for the development of self-governing institutions. This was a big step for both home rule leagues, but it didn't mean that India got its self-government. The British made sure to add a clause that only the British government had the power to decide when and under what conditions the self-rule would be granted.

However, the majority of members of the home rule leagues were pacified by the statement of Edwin Montagu, and they sought no further action. Instead of continuing its struggles, Annie Besant's home rule league dissolved. Even though she was promoted as the president of the Indian National Congress, her previous followers stopped attending the meetings in 1918. When the government published the intended reforms, it created another split in the Indian National Congress. Some wanted to accept what the government offered immediately, while others wanted to reject it all. Besant herself, even though she was aware of the need for further fighting, questioned the effectiveness of passive resistance. She also condemned the reforms the government offered, saying that they were an embarrassment for Britain; however, she later advocated in their favor.

Tilak was consistent in his beliefs, and he wanted to continue the fight for self-government, but he couldn't do it alone. He decided to leave for England at the end of 1918, where he sued Valentine Chirol for defamation. Tilak's absence from the political life of India during these critical months only sped up the demise of the league. Even though the league was short-lived, it did make a huge step for the self-governance of India. The members of both the Indian National Congress and the home rule leagues who remained true to their nationalistic ideology would prove to be the backbone of the movement under the leadership of Mahatma Gandhi, a man who was already famous for his efforts to improve the lives of Indians in South Africa.

Chapter 7 – Mahatma Gandhi

Photograph of Mahatma Gandhi taken in 1931

https://en.wikipedia.org/wiki/Mahatma_Gandhi#/media/File:Mahatma-Gandhi,_studio,_1931.jpg

In South Africa

An Indian lawyer, who studied in London, Mohandas Karamchand Gandhi is one of the most known people in the world. He was an Indian anti-colonialism activist and ethicist renowned for his nonviolent methods of resistance. Today, he is a symbol of pacifism and world peace, and he continues to inspire people all over the world to fight for their freedom and rights. He is well known by his honorable title Mahatma, which many confuse for his actual name. In Sanskrit, Mahatma means venerable, and he was first referred to as such during his activism in South Africa.

Indians had started their migration to South Africa during 1890, as the poverty and lack of work drove them to seek fortune beyond their homeland, mostly in other British colonies. Gandhi was invited to South Africa to represent an Indian merchant in a lawsuit. He was the first highly educated Indian to arrive in South Africa, and he chose to stay there and even bring his family with him. But young Gandhi was baffled by the racism he saw, which was a part of the everyday life of an Indian in South Africa. Gandhi was from a respected family, as his father was a dewan (state minister), and he couldn't swallow all the racial insults coming his way, either by the locals or by the white colonialists. Not even in England, where he spent three years studying, did he encounter such racism directed at him. Besides the usual verbal insults, Gandhi was denied entrance in the first-class carriage of a train, even though he had the appropriate ticket. He was instead directed to sit at the back of the train with the luggage. Another instance was at a hotel, where he had a room booked, but the management simply didn't believe him and kicked him out. He continued to experience such racist indecencies throughout his stay in South Africa.

Upon his arrival in Pretoria, where the trial was to take place, Gandhi immediately gathered his fellow Indians and offered to teach them English so they could get by in everyday life in a foreign country. He also suggested that they should oppose this oppression and organize some kind of protest against it. In addition, Gandhi voiced his displeasure through the press.

Gandhi didn't mean to settle in South Africa, and after the lawsuit was over, he prepared to go back to India. But the uneducated Indians begged him to stay at least for a month to help them organize their protests. Since they did not know the English language, they couldn't even draft the petitions, let alone understand more complicated documents. Gandhi agreed to stay for one month, but he ended up staying much longer. He arrived as a 25-year-old lawyer, and when he left, he was a 45-year-old Mahatma.

Gandhi's activism was mainly in the political sphere, as he sent numerous petitions and letters to South African legislatures, the colonial secretary in London, and to British Parliament. He was sure that the British government just needed to hear all the facts of the oppression of Indians in South Africa to make them intervene. To raise his effectiveness and unite the Indians from the worker and merchant classes, he founded the South African Indian Congress, and he also started his own newspaper, *Indian Opinion*. He was an efficient fundraiser, journalist, politician, and propagandist in one whole package. However, by 1906, Gandhi was completely convinced that the "moderate" methods he undertook were getting him nowhere.

From 1906 onward, Gandhi implemented his idea of passive resistance, which he named Satyagraha. The term itself is a combination of the Sanskrit words for "truth" and "insistence." But for Gandhi, satyagraha was more philosophical, as he explained that the truth is love and that the insistence is force. According to him, satyagraha is a "love force" that is strong enough to bring change. The core of Gandhi's philosophy was civil disobedience, although he preferred to call it "civil resistance." He preached that the best way to fight oppression was through nonviolent, passive resistance. However, this doesn't mean that the activists of satyagraha did nothing. The point was to refuse to obey the government as an alternative to violence.

For example, when the government in South Africa made it obligatory for all Indians to register and to carry their compulsory certificates of registration with them at all times, they refused to do so. When the government started prosecuting Indians for disobedience, they simply pleaded guilty and were sent to jail.

However, the number of Indians in jails steadily grew, as they insisted on practicing civil disobedience. In just a few weeks, the number of jailed Indians rose to 155, and they even mockingly called it "King Edward's Hotel." Finally, the government realized that their legislation had no effect, and they had to give in. A deal was made stating that the law would be withdrawn if Indians willingly registered themself. Gandhi was the first to accept these terms, proving that his satyagraha was successful.

However, the government played a trick on the Indian activists and passed another law that restricted Indian immigration to South Africa. Gandhi and his followers realized the fight would have to continue. To support the activists and their families, Gandhi opened the Tolstoy Farm, which was a donation from his rich German friend Hermann Kallenbach, who admired Gandhi's philosophy. The farm was set to offer sustenance to the families of those Indians who were imprisoned due to civil disobedience in their fight against the government. Named after Russian author Leo Tolstoy, who greatly influenced both Gandhi and Kallenbach, the farm was one of the first ashrams, which, in this case, were similar farms opened in India during the period of Gandhi's activism in his home country.

Gandhi's nonviolent satyagraha meant several imprisonments for both him and his followers. In South African jails, they were put through hard work, starvation, and beatings, and they were constantly kept in dark cells. But the struggle continued, and the harsh environment of the prison didn't break their spirits. Once the prison conditions became public, Indian workers all over South Africa went on strike. The satyagraha forced the government to sit with its opponents at a negotiation table, and many demands of the oppressed Indians in South Africa were met. Gandhi was satisfied with the actions of his people, and he felt like he had taught them everything his philosophy had to offer. It was time for him to go back home to India and bring satyagraha there.

In India

In January 1915, Mahatma Gandhi moved back to India, where he was received with a warm welcome. His deeds in South Africa were already known to his fellow Indians back home, and although he did expect some educated colleagues to know of his actions, he was not prepared for the masses of people who came to welcome him. One of the leaders of the Indian National Congress, Gopal Krishna Gokhale, described Gandhi as a man who was made out of the stuff of which heroes and martyrs were made. For Gokhale and many Indians who admired Gandhi, that stuff was his spirit, which he used to inspire the people around him.

But for a year after his arrival, Gandhi didn't join any political activities that would bring India closer to its independence. This is because he decided to spend as much time as he needed to study the situation of India. He traveled the subcontinent to see for himself how the communities lived and what demands Indians had. Everywhere he went, he would gain a horde of followers. However, his political views were different from those of the Indian National Congress and both home rule leagues. He did not join either of them, instead deciding to go a separate way.

During 1917 and 1918, Gandhi engaged himself in local political issues, and he was active during the three important struggles of Champaran (a city in Bihar), Ahmedabad, and Kheda (cities in Gujarat). Gandhi was arrested as soon as he entered Champaran, and he offered no resistance, confusing the politicians of India. He wasn't truly a rebel by their definition, even though he came to give his support to the peasants who fought against their landowners. Thus, the local authorities were ordered to release Gandhi. He proceeded with touring the villages and taking their statements to ensure a strong case against the system. But the government decided to convey an investigation and formed a Commission of Inquiry. They even invited Gandhi to be one of the members, and he used the gathered evidence from the peasants to persuade the commission that the workers had indeed been mistreated.

After the victory in Champaran, Gandhi went to Ahmedabad, where the industrial workers were protesting the mill owners, who wanted to take away the "plague bonus" from workers' payments because the plague had passed. However, the workers needed the bonus because the living expenses had increased during the outbreak of World War I. It was a British collector, a member of the British local administration, who asked Gandhi to come and propose a compromise between the workers and the mill owners. After his investigation, Gandhi concluded that the workers needed an increase in their salaries to meet the price demands of life during the world war. He suggested workers go on strike, and during it, Gandhi encouraged them by addressing them personally every day. Because there was a danger of starvation due to going on strike, as the workers no longer received their payments, Gandhi promised he would be the first to starve, and he committed himself to fast. The pressure on the mill owners was increased by Gandhi's fasting, and they finally agreed to meet the workers' demands.

In Kheda, the peasants had the same problems as those in Champaran, but here, they were caused by the failure of crops instead of the greed of landowners. The peasants demanded the remission of the land value, but the government ignored them. Gandhi couldn't allow the people to starve, and he called upon the law, which stated that if the crop yielded less than one-fourth of the average yearly harvest, the citizens were entitled to a total remission of the land revenue. However, all his appeals and petitions to the government failed, so he called upon the peasants to practice civil disobedience. The peasants of Kheda were too exhausted, though, as they had previously been stricken with the plague and now with hunger. The government agreed to collect the revenues only from those peasants who could pay but under the condition that it did not reach the public, as it would be a blow to the government's prestige.

Gandhi was compelled to agree to this condition due to the people's weak health. Even though there was no publicity given to his struggle in Kheda, Gandhi was victorious.

These three incidents were a demonstration of Gandhi's methods and their effectiveness. He also gained popularity while solving the problems of the common people around the country, and he now had the full knowledge to understand what the masses in India wanted, the masses that would be his weapon during the fight against colonial rule. The young people of India joined Gandhi's movement with every step he took. They loved how he was able to identify himself with the troubles of the common people and how he found strength and peace in pacifism.

In 1919, Gandhi already had enough followers to organize a massive protest against the British government, which planned to introduce unpopular legislation. As World War I was coming to an end, the British Raj planned to reduce the civil rights of their Indian subjects. Because of the threat that the nationalist movements in India presented, the British government wanted to extend the state of emergency that had been in place since the beginning of the war. This meant that the civil rights of a fair trial, imprisonment with defined accusations, and freedom of movement were to be restricted, if not completely taken away. These legislations were known as the Rowlatt Act, named after the president of the sedition committee who proposed them, Sidney Rowlatt.

After the protests failed, Gandhi proposed implementing his satyagraha. The younger members of the home rule leagues rushed to join Gandhi's movement, as they wanted to distance themselves from the government officials. They were the ones who reached out to their colleagues and created a huge network for spreading the propaganda of satyagraha. Gandhi's followers decided to organize a massive strike throughout the country, which would include fasting and praying.

The nationwide satyagraha was launched on April 6th, 1919, but there was some confusion with the date in some parts of India, as Delhi held their strike on March 30th. There was also a lot of violence on the streets of the city, which was against everything that satyagraha stood for. Violence spread through other cities, and it culminated in Punjab, where the people had suffered the most during the war. They had been hit by diseases, hunger, and excessive recruitment for the war. Gandhi tried to reach Punjab and pacify its people, but the British government deported him to Bombay. Since Bombay was in flames too, he decided to stay there and help calm down the situation.

In the city of Amritsar in Punjab, the situation escalated to include some very tragic events. The locals started attacking British citizens, including women and children. Because of the violence, the government decided to call in the army and hand the city to General Reginald Dyer, who immediately took action by prohibiting public meetings. However, April 13th was the festival of Vaisakhi, which both Sikhs and Hindus celebrate. A large crowd of people gathered to observe the holiday, and even the peasants from neighboring villages flocked to the city. This was in direct defiance to General Dyer's orders, and he ordered his troops to start shooting at the unarmed crowd for a full ten minutes. He didn't even warn the people, who were trapped, as the city was walled, offering no place to run or hide. The official count was 379 dead, but unofficial numbers go much higher. Over 1,000 people were injured. The youngest victim of what became known as the Amritsar massacre was a six-week-old baby. The Indian National Congress decided to investigate the casualties for themselves, as the numbers offered by the British government did not match the number of fires shot and the number of attendants, which was roughly around 20,000. They concluded that around 1,000 people were killed, with 500 dying later due to the wounds they had received.

Even though the massacre stunned the whole nation, the situation in Punjab only got worse. Martial law was in effect, and so, the people were put through various indignities, such as being forced to crawl on their bellies and to kiss the boots of the Europeans. The brutality that took place in Punjab made Gandhi and his followers withdraw their strike. However, Mahatma Gandhi didn't lose faith in his people. Only a year later, he started another nationwide strike, and the Amritsar massacre was just one of the reasons for its launch.

The Non-cooperation Movement

The Amritsar massacre and the increased violence in Punjab horrified Gandhi, and he made a promise that if India united in the efforts of nonviolent protests, the Swaraj (self-government) would come in a year. He didn't believe anymore in the good intentions of the British, as no government could commit such a crime on its subjects and be willing to make changes for the better. But Gandhi was the only one who was revolted by the actions of the British government. The First World War had just ended, and the people realized that the British had made many post-war promises that they had no intention of keeping. The people were still as hungry as they were during the war, they still died of preventable diseases due to the poor healthcare system, and they were still treated as uncivilized subhumans by the Europeans.

But one of the promises that Britain didn't keep after the war brought about the wrath of the Muslims, who finally joined Gandhi's movement. The British had promised that after the world war, the Ottoman Caliphate would be restored. The Ottoman rulers were considered to be the leaders of the Sunni faith and politics. The Treaty of Sèvres, signed a few years after the end of the First World War in 1920, partitioned the Ottoman Empire and the Sunni Caliphate, which only angered the Muslims in India. In protest of the Treaty of Sèvres, the Indian Muslims organized a movement of their own, known as the Khilafat movement. Gandhi was sympathetic to their cause and invited them to join other Indians in protest against the British Raj, which the members of the Khilafat movement gladly accepted.

Even the Indian National Congress agreed that not much could be achieved through constitutional means, and many members joined Gandhi's non-cooperation movement. They called upon their colleagues to not comply with the legislative matters of the British government and to withdraw from the upcoming parliamentary elections. Even the voters refused to vote. Some of the Congress members didn't agree with the decision to boycott elections, but under the pressure of their party, they complied and withdrew. Annie Besant supported India's fight for self-governance, but she didn't agree with the socialist ideas. She left the Congress and continued to advocate India's independence on her own, through various campaigns both in India and in England.

Formally, the movement was launched on August 1st with a nationwide protest (hartal) taking place. On the same day, in the early morning hours, Bal Gangadhar Tilak died, and many people began fasting and praying as they mourned his passing. Some scholars place September 4th as the official date when the non-cooperation movement was launched, as that is the day the Indian National Congress joined the movement. By December, the members of the Congress decided to surrender all of their honors and titles and boycott British schools, laws, clothing, and taxes.

Congress worked on opening Indian schools, and they also founded Panchayats, which are local self-governments that have the authority to settle disputes. Members of Congress also encouraged the domestic production of textiles and asked all Hindus and Muslims to live in unity and give up the practice of untouchability. The nationwide movement for nonviolent disobedience was set in place, and even the extreme revolutionary terrorists from Bengal joined the movement and stopped their guerilla attacks.

During 1921, Gandhi and the leaders of the Khilafat movement went on a national tour of the country, organizing many gatherings with various politicians and addressing the common people personally. In the first month alone, their movement influenced around 90,000 students to leave British schools and enroll in newly opened national schools. Lawyers even refused to enter courts and follow the British laws, sacrificing their lucrative careers. This served to inspire more people to join the movement.

However, it seems that the boycott of British textiles and clothing had the most effect. Volunteers were organized, and they went from house to house to collect all foreign clothing, which they burned in a bonfire. They didn't burn only the clothes, as the boycott expanded to include all foreign products. Government revenues that were brought about by selling foreign products in India declined so much that the British were forced to implement new propaganda that would persuade Indians that foreign goods were beneficial to them. However, this propaganda had little effect.

Mohammed Ali Jauhar, one of the leaders of the Khilafat movement, was arrested after he made a statement that it went against Islam to serve in the British Army and that all Muslim sepoys should immediately leave. Gandhi supported Jauhar, and he issued a manifesto in which he repeated Jauhar's words. Gandhi also made a call to all Indian soldiers of any religion to sever their ties with the British Army. The Indian National Congress adopted the same resolution and continued to spread propaganda among the Indian soldiers. The British government was essentially powerless, and they couldn't do anything to persuade the Indians to join their army. It was the first victory of the non-cooperation movement, as the British government had to capitulate and take the blow to its prestige. The second blow occurred when the prince of Wales, Edward VIII, visited India. He landed in Bombay and planned a public tour of the city. However, all the streets were empty on that day, and all the windows had their shutters down.

Despite the successes that the non-cooperation movement achieved with its use of nonviolence, Indians around the country were somehow inspired to turn to aggression. At first, the violent acts were small and didn't cause much trouble with the local authorities, but Gandhi was worried that the movement would turn away from his pacifist views. The British government didn't take any actions against the movement in the beginning, thinking it would quickly pass. But when the Khilafat leaders started openly talking about violence during their meetings, the government decided to act. They started arresting all the leaders of both the Khilafat movement and Congress. Soon, the leaders of the non-cooperation movement were arrested as well, and only Gandhi was still free. The government proclaimed any large gatherings of people to be illegal, and they started raids on the offices and homes of the movement's officials. In total, 30,000 people were arrested around the country.

Gandhi had no other choice but to call for nationwide civil disobedience once again, as his pleas to Rufus Isaacs, the viceroy of India, to release the political prisoners were ignored. However, on February 5th, 1922, the civil disobedience turned into another massacre, this time in the small town of Chauri Chaura in the United Provinces. There, the protesters attacked the policemen who tried to stop their picketing of a liquor shop. A conflict between the protesters and police broke out, which led to a police station being set on fire with 22 officers still inside. Gandhi was revolted by this incident, and he called off the movement. He even persuaded the Indian National Congress to ratify his decision. Single-handedly, Gandhi had ended the non-cooperation movement on February 15th, 1922. He was arrested on March 10th and sentenced to six years of imprisonment on the charges of sedition.

Gandhi was released from prison due to his declining health on February 5th, 1924. The new nationalist political party, the Swaraj Party, had already been constructed out of the remnants of the Indian National Congress and the non-cooperation movement. But they had a different agenda than the nonviolent approach of their predecessors. Their plan was not to boycott the British government but to enter and bring it down from within. Gandhi didn't agree with the new methods the nationalists had in mind, but he also didn't stand in their way. The years between 1922 and 1927 were years of separate activism movements, each working for its own agenda. However, no results were achieved, and the atmosphere of apathy and frustration prevailed in all the nationalist organizations. It seemed as if they all needed a break to rest and recoup.

However, this doesn't mean that the whole of India stopped its resistance to British rule. There were many movements on the rise that tell their own stories, but they all ultimately failed. Some of them won small victories but led India no closer to its independence. The revolutionary terrorists were also on the rise with guerilla warfare in the Bengal province. But government actions decimated their numbers, and with the death of their leader in 1931, the revolutionary movement came to an end. The revolutionaries didn't have a clear political plan, and because of that, they were unable to move the masses and gain their trust. However, their willingness to sacrifice themselves did touch the Indian nation and inspired them to take action once more. Indians were reminded of their nationalism and patriotic sentiment, and they were ready to take the fight into their own hands.

The Salt March

The Salt March led by Gandhi

https://upload.wikimedia.org/wikipedia/commons/thumb/7/7c/Marche_sel.jpg/1280px-Marche_sel.jpg

The Swaraj Party fell apart after the death of its leader, Chittaranjan Das, in 1925. The Indian National Congress reorganized itself, and they rose in protest when the British government decided to form a commission that would look at the Indian constitution and make changes. The problem was that the commission was composed only of Europeans. Since Sir John Simon was at its head, it is remembered as the Simon Commission. The Indians were outraged that they were not even considered for such a task, and the organized protests only grew in power after the freedom fighter Lala Lajpat Rai died due to severe beatings by the police.

As a response to the Simon Commission, the Indian National Congress appointed its own members to form a similar commission and propose their changes to the British government. The idea was to give India self-government within the British Empire, but the British decided to ignore both the Congress and their commission. As a result, the Congress only grew in its determination, and once the negotiations with the government failed, they brought up the declaration of India's independence, known as Purna Swaraj (complete self-rule).

On December 31st, 1929, the new president of the Congress, Jawaharlal Nehru, hoisted the flag of India in Lahore. They proclaimed January 26th as the Independence Day of India, and the Indian flag was displayed throughout the whole subcontinent. In February 1930, the Congress asked Gandhi to launch a civil disobedience movement, giving him all the power to decide the time, place, and the political program of it. Gandhi chose the British government's salt laws as the first issue that the movement would address.

The Salt Act of 1882 instituted a British monopoly on salt gathering, production, and distribution. The taxes they imposed were too high for the common people of India to pay, and according to the Salt Act, any intent to acquire salt by any other means was a criminal offense. Even though Indians could have produced their own salt easily by evaporating seawater, they were prohibited from doing so.

The Indian National Congress thought the salt laws were not a good starting point, as they couldn't see how a protest against it would affect the government. Indeed, even the viceroy of India, Lord Edward Irwin, thought the announced protests wouldn't give him too much trouble, and the British government openly laughed at Gandhi's idea. However, Gandhi had a good reason for choosing the salt laws. Salt was a commodity everyone needed, for without it, life would be impossible. Thus, the protest against the British monopoly on salt was a thing that concerned all the people of India, every caste, every religion, and every individual, no matter their age. Gandhi knew that if he organized a political protest with ideas such as civil rights, the common people wouldn't respond as readily, as politics were an abstract idea for the majority of them.

Gandhi's belief of nonviolence and his philosophy of satyagraha led him to choose a march as his first means of civil disobedience in his fight against the salt laws. He notified the viceroy of India about the details of his march, and the first reports of Gandhi's intentions to defy the salt laws were published in the press on February 5th, 1930. Gandhi invited media from all over the world to announce the march, and he often held vigorous speeches insisting on the importance of nonviolence and civil disobedience. On March 2nd, he wrote again to Viceroy Lord Irwin, asking him to meet his demands of, among others, land revenue assessments, cutting military spending, and the abolishment of the salt tax. He even promised he would withdraw from the announced march, but the viceroy ignored him.

Gandhi's march began on March 12th in Sabarmati Ashram, the suburbs of Ahmedabad. Eighty of his followers from Sabarmati Ashram designated as his marching companions, and they were chosen because they were representatives of various castes and were trained in Gandhi's satyagraha. The route of the march was well planned, and the procession was to visit 48 villages that had been specifically chosen because of their recruitment potential. The Salt March lasted for 24 days and ended in Dandi, Gujarat. On his way, Gandhi walked 240 miles (390 kilometers), stopping in each village to hold a speech to inspire more people to join him. Soon, he was followed by thousands of people, all wearing white clothes, which was why the march was named "White Flowing River." Gandhi never stopped giving interviews for the media that followed him, and he even wrote his own articles and news reports. The *New York Times* wrote about Gandhi's progression daily, while many foreign news companies chose to shoot newsreel footage.

The Salt March ended on April 6th when the procession reached the seashore. There, Gandhi raised a hunk of salty mud from the ground and boiled it in seawater, producing illegal salt. With this act, he officially started the civil disobedience movement. He instructed his followers to produce illegal salt wherever it was possible, and this movement is often seen as the start of the fall of the British rule in

India. Chakravarti Rajagopalachari organized his own salt march on the east coast. At the end of his route, he was arrested by the British authorities.

Gandhi anticipated the police to arrest him as well, but it didn't happen. The British government was confused by the peaceful disobedience and didn't know how to react. They preferred an enemy who fought back and had no idea how to fight nonviolence. A month later, Mahatma Gandhi was arrested and accused of instigating protests. But the government reaction came too late, as the civil disobedience movement had already spread throughout the country. Peasants refused to pay taxes, illegal salt was being produced and sold everywhere, and a new wave of boycotts of foreign products started.

Unfortunately, in some provinces, violence erupted. However, unlike during the non-cooperation movement, Gandhi did not withdraw. He condemned the violence and advocated for its end, but he was committed to the movement. The violence culminated in Peshawar, where British soldiers fired on a crowd that was peacefully protesting the arrest of their leader, Abdul Ghaffar Khan. Around 200 unarmed Indian protesters lost their lives.

Gandhi succeeded in his attempt to make the salt laws into a cause that would shake the whole nation. After his arrest, people became ever more innovative in coming up with different forms of civil disobedience. Boycotts of everything foreign began anew, and this time, women were leaders. Never before did India see the raw strength of their women. Even those who covered their faces with veils in the practice of purdah (the seclusion of females in Muslim and Hindu cultures) stood strong in front of the various storefronts that sold British goods, successfully changing the minds of both buyers and shopkeepers. Gandhi admired women, and his philosophy promoted more freedom for females; however, it should be noted that he was a conservative in a gentler form. He believed that a woman should only get an education that would help her play the traditional role of a mother and wife.

While Indians nonviolently and effectively protested all over the subcontinent, the British government sought ways to achieve some kind of compromise with the people. Gandhi was invited to a Round Table Conference in London in 1930, where the talks about the Indian constitution were to happen. But once he was there, he was told not to expect to talk about the independence of India. Even though the conference was ultimately unsuccessful for the Indians, the conference was still the first event in history in which the British and Indians sat at a table as equals. When Gandhi returned home, the British released all of the political prisoners of the civil disobedience movement. On March 5th, 1931, Gandhi and Viceroy Lord Irwin signed a truce known as the Gandhi-Irwin Pact. The British monopoly on salt production and trade was lifted, meaning Indians could legally make, sell, and buy their own salt again.

The Salt March remains one of the most important moments in human history. It is estimated that around 90,000 Indians were arrested during the protests that followed. The Salt March also inspired the fight against oppressive regimes all around the world. In the US, Martin Luther King Jr. admired Gandhi's idea of uniting the people around a common cause. In South Africa, Nelson Mandela used some of the satyagraha methods while overthrowing the apartheid system. People of all nations around the world still use peaceful, nonviolent protests to voice their disagreements with the acts of their governments.

Chapter 8 – World War II, the "Quit India" Movement, and Independence

Indian soldiers in Burma

https://en.wikipedia.org/wiki/India_in_World_War_II#/media/File:INDIAN_TROOPS_IN_BURMA,_1944.jpg

World War II is generally thought to have started when the German forces invaded Poland on September 1st, 1939. The first to respond were France and the United Kingdom. Although the first battles were fought on European soil, India, under the rule of the British Raj, joined the war just a few days after its start. The Indian viceroy at the time, Lord Linlithgow, didn't even bother to consult with the leading Indian politicians or listen to public opinion. Instead, he declared that India would fight on the side of Britain, undermining the previous efforts of India to gain its independence. The faraway war took over 2.5 million soldiers from India, who defended the territories of other British colonies, such as Singapore and Hong Kong. The Indian soldiers also fought in the territories of Europe and Africa–they went pretty much wherever the Allies needed them. During the war, the British government led India into debt by taking a couple of billion pounds from India, which was needed to finance the war. The measures the British implemented within India were so oppressive that they directly caused the Bengal famine of 1943, which they declined to implement a relief program for. In Burma and British Malaya, the European soldiers and inhabitants of these colonies were safely evacuated, leaving the locals and Indian soldiers to fend for themselves.

The biggest political party of India at the time was the Indian National Congress, whose leadership was entrusted to Mahatma Gandhi, Maulana Abul Kalam Azad, and Vallabhbhai Patel (more commonly known as Sardar Patel). They agreed to decline help to the British government during the Second World War, even though they personally condemned the actions of Nazi Germany and Adolf Hitler. They promised their help only under the condition that India gained its independence. The British were not expecting the Indian National Congress to react this way, and they were baffled by their decision. However, India wasn't united in their decision to decline help to the British. The All-India Muslim League and some of the smaller political parties actually gave their support to the British government. But the Congress demanded that Britain transfer all its governmental power to them. Unable to comply, the two found themselves in a stalemate. The provincial governments failed due to the mass resignation of the members of the Congress, and the probability of a nationwide revolt became very real.

The British government continued its efforts to persuade the Indian National Congress to find common ground. But all the negotiations failed, and time was running out, as Japan declared war on the Dutch and Britain in December 1941. The British defeat in Singapore, which Japan took over in February 1942, was a great blow to the British government's confidence. Some Indian politicians saw Japan's entry into the war as an opportunity. Subhas Chandra Bose, for instance, thought he could give his support to Japan and Germany and use their help to get rid of British rule. He founded the Indian National Army with Japan, which fought against the Allies. Afraid of the consequences of Bose's actions and after the loss of Singapore, the British government was forced to react.

British Prime Minister Winston Churchill sent Sir Stafford Cripps to negotiate for the pan-Indian support for the war in April 1942. For this, Cripps needed to get the Congress leaders and the All-India Muslim League to agree. Cripps belonged to a political party that supported Indian self-governance, and he did bring this promise to the negotiating table. However, the All-India Muslim League wanted a separate Muslim state after the war. It was impossible to satisfy both the Indian National Congress and the All-India Muslim League. On top of that, Churchill wasn't satisfied with Cripps's proposal that India should gain the status of a dominion (semi-independent states). The negotiations quickly fell apart, and Sir Stafford Cripps had no other choice but to proclaim his mission as a failure.

After unsuccessful negotiations with the British diplomat, it became clear to the Indian National Congress that Britain had no intention of letting India go. India's unwilling partnership in World War II was to be continued, which went against everything that Gandhi's satyagraha stood for. Even though he didn't want to do anything that would obstruct the British efforts against Nazi Germany, Gandhi finally realized that it was impossible to stay silent and let the Allies and the Axis Powers divide India for their own use. He spent the spring drafting a resolution for the Congress that called for Britain's departure from India and the adoption of nonviolent methods in their efforts against Japan. By August 1942, the Indian National Congress adopted this resolution, and the movement became known as "Quit India," after the slogan that followed it, "Bharat Chhodo."

Mahatma Gandhi made a very powerful speech on the eve of the creation of the "Quit India" movement. He called for passive resistance and made a comparison with the French and Russian revolutions, saying that they failed in their achievement of democratic ideals because they were fought with weapons. India was to gain its freedom by nonviolence. However, the slogan he gave to the people was "do or die," which he interpreted as the will to persist in their efforts until India finally became independent. In his words, Indians would rather die than endure everlasting slavery to the British Raj.

Instructing his people in nonviolent disobedience, Gandhi asked them to wait for the official launch of the movement, as he wanted to give one more chance to the viceroy of India to accept their terms. But the government was in no mood to negotiate again. Instead, on August 9th, they launched a series of arrests targeted at the leaders and members of the Indian National Congress, as well as anyone who opposed their rule. Around 90,000 people were arrested in a single swipe, as the British were anticipating some kind of revolution. However, these government actions backfired, as they did not foresee the aggressive reactions of the Indians to these arrests. The leaderless people managed to gather and oppose local authorities in response to the arrests. Bombay, Ahmedabad, and Pune were the first to rise, and only a few days later, Delhi, Allahabad, Kanpur, and Patna, among others, joined in. The people openly defied the British laws and organized hartals, mass protests, in cities and towns around India.

To stop the spreading unrest, the British government banned all press from reporting about the "Quit India" movement. However, only the *National Herald* and *Harijan* ceased writing about the struggle during its duration. Gandhi himself was arrested, but he made sure to leave behind written instructions on how to peacefully disobey the British rule. He proposed that students should leave their studies, that workers should strike, and that villagers should stop paying taxes. He also invited the people of the princely states to join the rest of India and for the princes to abandon their support of the British government. However, it was the common people who proved to be the most imaginative in disobeying the laws. The symbols of the governmental rule, such as railway stations, police stations, and courts, were constantly under attack. Indians would hoist the national flag of India on these buildings to demonstrate their anger. The villagers would also gather in groups of hundreds and dismantle the nearby railroads. Bridges were blown up, and telephone and telegraph lines were cut. All of these were the symbols of British rule, and the people felt the need to get rid of them.

Students quit their studies as Gandhi proposed and devoted their time to volunteering in the movement by spreading the news all around India. They printed illegal newspapers, which they would then distribute to nearby villages, calling on the peasants to join the uprising. Students also acted as couriers for the underground network of rebels that organized worker strikes all over the subcontinent. It was the students who called for the burning of police and railway stations and who hijacked the local trains to paint them in the national colors of India. The movement was the strongest in Bihar, where for two weeks, no government authority existed, as the officials had fled from the angry populace. Unfortunately, the people of India indulged in violence, and some European civilians were attacked. As Gandhi later explained, Indians couldn't differentiate between the British Empire and the British people. To them, they were one and the same. Fighting one meant fighting the other, and a number of British who lived in India died.

The British government did not sit idle, and the suppression of the uprisings was installed almost immediately. The police freely shot at the unarmed crowds of demonstrators, and the government also approved of low-flying aircraft machine-gunning civilians. The hostages the British captured were taken from their villages, and collective fines were imposed on disobedient settlements. In some cases, the government burned whole villages down if they suspected they were hiding resistance fighters. Even though martial law wasn't proclaimed, the army was free to do whatever they wanted. The soldiers would beat citizens, often torturing and killing them whenever they had the opportunity. The mass gatherings and violence against the government symbols stopped after six weeks of brutal repression. However, the movement continued to operate underground.

The British government called on Gandhi to condemn the violence of the people, but he refused to do so, saying that the fault lay with the British rule, not the people. Furthermore, on February 10th, 1943, he started a fast while in jail as a reply to the government's efforts to belittle him. The news of Gandhi's fast quickly spread around the country, and once more, the subcontinent turned to protests, strikes, and demonstrations. Prisoners of various jails throughout India sympathized with the leader of the "Quit India" movement and went on hunger strikes of their own.

The people of India gathered in masses to demand Gandhi's release from prison. Some even traveled to openly protest in front of Aga Khan Palace, where Gandhi was detained. Soon enough, word spread around the world, and people from various countries bombarded the British government of India with letters and telegraphs demanding his release. The press joined the call, and newspapers such as the *Chicago Sun*, *News Chronicle*, and

Manchester Guardian openly challenged the British Raj. Various local and world organizations followed suit, including the British Communist Party, the Women's International League, the Australian Council of Trade Unions, and even the United States government. However, the British government, under the leadership of Prime Minister Churchill, was unmoved. A feeling that the "Quit India" movement had failed spread throughout the nation. As a result, morale slowly declined as it seemed that the people had given up.

Gandhi was to remain in prison until May 6th, 1944, when he was finally released because of his weakened health. With his release, the struggle for India's independence continued with renewed vigor. Gandhi mostly focused on uniting the Indian people under the same cause. Although there would always be supporters of the British Raj among the locals, their numbers were getting smaller by each passing month. By 1945, the national support for India's independence outgrew the area ruled by the British Raj. The slow repatriation of foreign soldiers who had served in India during World War II led to several mutinies in the army. Even though these mutinies were quickly suppressed, it became clear to all parties where the support of the whole nation was. The same year, Clement Attlee, who had argued for India's independence since the beginning of his political career, became Britain's new prime minister. He organized the Cabinet Mission, whose sole purpose was to peacefully transfer governmental powers to India.

However, the problem of Pakistan remained. Muslims wanted their own state, while the Indian National Congress advocated for a united Indian state. The British believed that an election would settle this issue, and it was held in December 1945. The Indian National Congress won 59 governmental seats, while the All-India Muslim League won 30. The Europeans got eight, and the rest was divided between the smaller parties. However, Muslims continued to demand separation. To appease them, the Cabinet Mission came up with the plan in which India would remain united but with internal state groupings, which would allow Muslims to have autonomy within the provinces where they ruled. The All-India Muslim League agreed to these terms, but the Indian National Congress rejected them, fearing it would weaken their hold on the whole subcontinent. Angered, the Muslims started protesting and even attacked Hindus in Calcutta. The Hindus answered the violence with more violence, and what is known as the "Great Calcutta Killing of 1946" occurred, where around 4,000 people lost their lives.

When the British prime minister appointed Lord Louis Mountbatten as the last viceroy of India with the task of overseeing the transition of power to an independent India by 1948, the leaders of the Indian National Congress pursued ways to speed up the process. They accepted the partition that the Muslims wanted, and they also sought ways to stop the violence that had spread from Calcutta to other regions of India. The fear of a Hindu-Muslim civil war led other Congress leaders to accept the partition as well.

Gandhi, however, opposed the partition, as he felt it went against all of his beliefs of a united India that would accept different religions. In spite of this, other leaders agreed that Pakistan already existed within India and that to ignore it would only lead to even more violence. The Partition Council was formed in 1947, and the division of public assets began. The areas and territories that were predominantly populated by Hindus and Sikhs were to belong to the new India, while predominantly Muslim areas were to become Pakistan. The provinces of Punjab and Bengal had to be divided between the two states, as they had mixed populations of both Muslims and Hindus. However, this didn't go peacefully. Violence erupted in the areas that were to be the new borders, a kind of violence that none of the politicians foresaw. Exhausted by World War II and unable to deal with the civil war that was rising in India, Britain decided to speed up the independence of the nation. August 14th, 1947, is the official date of the birth of the Dominion of

Pakistan, with its dominion status ending in 1956. On August 15th, 1947, India gained its independence. The British Raj was no more.

Conclusion

The departure of Britain left India in a state of civil war. Violence emerging on the borderlines of the two new states resulted in many Hindu and Muslim refugees who needed new homes. Gandhi continued to work for the good of his people and eventually came to terms with the partition. Unfortunately, the killings happened on both sides of the new border, and the death rate is calculated to be between 200,000 and 2 million. The resettlement of the refugees lasted until 1951, and the city of Delhi took in most of them. With that move, its population spiked, and it remains one of the most populated cities in the world. Hindus continue to migrate to India to this day due to the religious persecutions they are exposed to in Pakistan. The partition of the Indian subcontinent is still one of the most controversial events of the 20th century.

Mahatma Gandhi was assassinated on January 30th, 1948, and his killer, Nathuram Godse, claims he did it because he blamed Gandhi for all the violence that happened due to the partition. He belonged to the extremist Hindu Mahasabha party, which believed that Gandhi was too compliant with the Muslims.

Once India became an independent state, the decision was made to keep British political ideologies intact, such as democracy, the rule of law, and, to some extent, the equality of people. Some of the institutions founded by the British Raj and the ideas behind them remain active to this day. The universities and colleges, the stock exchange, and civil services still function, for the most part, as they did before.

But what of all the British people who had built their lives in India? Where are they now? Most of them left, but some decided to stay. Many had Indian wives and children, and as such, they couldn't simply leave. Some continued to work for the Indian government, while some chose to retire and spend their days with their families. They had to adjust to the new situation the best they could. However, most of them had to leave anyways. This was not because they were expelled out of the country but because their duties called them back home. The cultural transition these individuals had to undergo left a deep scar on their personalities. Life in India was very different than that in Britain. Many of them also left behind their Indian lovers, wives, and children to return to British wives and legitimate offspring. Some returned with opium addictions, while others couldn't cope with the depression that followed, a depression caused by the abandonment of the only lives they knew.

As the British Raj left its mark on the Indian subcontinent, the people who returned to Britain were permanently marked by the lives they had once led in India.

References

Bengal Famine Code. National Institute of Public Administration, Dacca University Campus, 1967.

Beveridge, Henry. *A Comprehensive History of India, Civil, Military and Social, from the First Landing of the English, to the Suppression of the Sepoy Revolt; Including an Outline of the Early History of Hindoostan.* Blackie and Son, 1880.

Foster, William, and Patrick J. N. Tuck. *The East India Company: 1600-1858.* Routledge, 1998.

Gandhi, and Gopal Gandhi. *The Oxford India Gandhi: Essential Writings.* Oxford University Press, 2008.

Golant, William. *The British Raj.* 1988.

Sharma, Sanjay. *Famine, Philanthropy and the Colonial State: North India in the Early Nineteenth Century.* Oxford University Press, 2001.

Shastitko Petr Mikhaĭlovich., and Savitri Shahani. *Nana Sahib: An Account of the People's Revolt in India, 1857-1859.* Shubhada Saraswat Publications, 1980.

Avasthy, R. S. (1967). *The Mughal Emperor Humayun.* Allahabad: History Dept., University of Allahabad.

Losty, J. P., & Roy, M. (2012). *Mughal India: Art, Culture and Empire: Manuscripts and Paintings in the British Library.* London: The British Library.
Ojha, P. N. (1979). *Glimpses of Social life in Mughal India.* New Delhi: Classical Publications.
Richards, J. (1996). *The Mughal Empire.* Cambridge: Cambridge University Press.
Sarkar, J. (1932). *Fall of the Mughal Empire.* Calcutta: M.C. Sarkar.
Sezgin, F., 'Amāwī Māzin, Ehrig-Eggert, C., & Neubauer, E. (1997). *Mughal India according to European travel accounts: texts and studies.* Frankfurt am Main: Institute for the History of Arabic-Islamic Science.
Shashi, S. S. (1999). *Babar: The First Mughal Emperor of India.* New Delhi: Anmol Publications.

Here's another book by Captivating History that you might be interested in

CPSIA information can be obtained
at www.ICGtesting.com
Printed in the USA
BVHW082346191221
624489BV00001B/61